# The Flying Boy
## Healing
## The Wounded Man

John H. Lee

Health Communications, Inc.
Deerfield Beach, Florida

John Lee
Austin Men's Center
Austin, Texas

**Library of Congress Cataloging-in-Publication Data**

Lee, John, 1951-
  The flying boy.

  Reprint. Originally published: S.L.: New Men's Press, 1987.
  1. Men—Psychology. 2. Emotions—Case studies.
3. Grief—Case studies. 4. Interpersonal relations—
Case studies. 5. Self-actualization (Psychology)—
Case studies. I. Title.
BF692.5.I43   1989            155.6'32            88-24466
ISBN 1-55874-006-6

Published by: Health Communications, Inc.
              3201 S.W. 15th Street
              Deerfield Beach, Florida 33442

# DEDICATION

For a special woman I love
and who unconditionally loved me

For my father and mother

For a special teacher, Robert Bly

# ACKNOWLEDGMENTS

I wish words could fully express my gratitude to the people who have helped me make this healing journey and write this book about it. My very special thanks to: Marilyn Yank who listened, cared deeply and was not afraid of the many tears; Dr. Bill Stott for being a great teacher and friend — he believed in my writing and my story when I could not; Dr. Betty Sue Flowers who gently guided and pushed me to tell my story in my own way; Dan Jones who has such a specialness in the way he counsels, befriends and edits; Dr. Mary Sue Moore for the patience of Job, her excellent therapy skills and concern; Melvin Kenne who listened, read, edited and quietly cared; Margie Downs for taking a heavy weight off my hands by using her own loving hands to type this manuscript; and many thanks to John Hunger, Ariana Vincent and Allen Maurer for editing, assisting and believing in me enough to spend many hours nurturing me and this book.

And thanks to many other people: my friends, clients and students who shared, listened and genuinely cared.

> . . . I believe one has to stop holding back for fear of alienating some imaginary reader or real relative or friend, and come out with personal truth. If we are to understand the human condition, and if we are to accept ourselves in all the complexity, self-doubt, extravagance of feeling, guilt, joy, the slow freeing of the self to its full capacity for action and creation, both as human being and as artist, we have to know all we can about each other, and we have to be willing to go naked.
>
> *Mary Sarton*

# FOREWORD TO THE
# SECOND EDITION

Many smiles have been smiled, feelings have been felt and wounds have been healed since I first wrote this book. Both book and I have changed. The book has changed from one that is only on "men's issues" and "masculine psychology" to one that crosses gender, cultural and sexual boundaries. Hundreds of women have said that "my" story is their story, too. People from Mexico, Canada and England have written that Flying Boys and Girls live in their countries, and Gay men and women feel this book speaks to them, too.

I have changed, too. When I wrote this book, I did not know what co-dependency really meant. Like many Adult Children of Alcoholics, I kept running away from anything to do with ACoA and found lots of reasons why the 12-Step programs would not work for me. This is no longer the case. The 12-Step meetings have helped my recovery greatly.

Shortly after this book was first published, a founding member of Co-dependents Anonymous called me. Although my book did not use the word "co-dependency", she recommended it to both her clients and fellow board members of Co-dependents Anonymous. Before her call, I had begun attending CODA meetings here in Austin. Thanks to CODA and the growing body of literature, I finally see that co-dependency and my adult child issues have been my problems all along. I realize now virtually all my relationships had been deeply dysfunctional, co-dependent and addictive. I was using people, relationships and work as drugs to keep me from feeling and remembering the painful traumas of childhood. My co-dependency and addictions allowed me to survive life but kept me from experiencing and living life fully and joyfully.

From one adult child of a dysfunctional family to another, I offer you a record of my journey into recovery. By reading my book, I hope you will find the missing pieces of your own life's puzzle. They will add to the big picture and thus your own recovery process. Together, we can make the journey out of co-dependency and addictive relationships and create healthy relationships with ourselves, our inner child, each other and our Higher Power.

God Bless.
John

# TABLE OF CONTENTS

# TABLE OF CONTENTS

# PREFACE

When I was 30, I was given an interview with the well-known American poet, Robert Bly. He has been instrumental in reviving in our culture an awareness of the "Goddess" within. He is now doing workshops and weekend retreats in which men come together to get in touch with their feelings of grief, anger, rage and, most important, their own rejected masculinity.

In 1981 I read one of the first articles about Robert Bly's work with men in *New Age Magazine*. While I was moved and completely understood what he was saying, several years passed before I felt the truth told by the man who spoke to me as one who had lived my life. His father was an alcoholic — so was mine. His mother treated him like a magic person and gave him what C.G. Jung terms a "mother complex" — so did mine. He had escaped the world of men — so had I. He said that men who didn't get in touch with their own deep masculinity found themselves unable to make commitments, hold down jobs and have good relationships. They constantly projected their souls onto the women they loved and left. These men did not have male friends because they only trusted females. He called them "Flying Boys" — I was a Flying Boy.

Unconsciously I had denied many things masculine and male in me. Though I looked and dressed like a lumberjack, I kept my hair long like my mother's. I saw maleness as exhibited by my drunken angry father and wanted no part of such meanness. I had seen maleness via the cultural fathers who sent their sons to Vietnam to live out their and John Wayne's dream of heroism and cultural domination. I wanted nothing to do with such maleness. I looked toward the "feminine" and tried to look like a "sensitive" man who would not use his intuition to plough through people's souls and bodies. My spirituality was deeply feminine and finally soft. During my early 30s, thanks to Bly, Laural and others, I realized that I was one who was completely out of balance and quickly approaching a "sickness unto death".

# INTRODUCTION

If you fly away from commitments, responsibilities, intimacy, feelings, male friendships and your own body, chances are you are a Flying Boy. If you are a woman reading this, chances are you have loved or come in contact with a Flying Boy.

Flying Boys frequently use fantasy to escape reality. They hide in their mind/intellect/reason to avoid the pain they keep in their bodies. They appear to all but those closest to them as sensitive, gentle and completely in touch with their feelings. The truth, except in the most extreme circumstances, is that they seldom even know they have bodies and feelings.

Fate and circumstance always seem to be controlling their lives. They can't quite make life work for themselves. When things do begin to work out or they finally succeed at something, they fly off in pursuit of another city, lover, job, degree, religion or drug.

Flying Boys are often addicted to sex, work, pain and failure as much as they are to intensity and darkness. They are constantly coming down from ecstatic highs and descending into deep, dramatic depressions. They seek the extremes and are bored with the in-between times.

Flying Boys often grew up in dysfunctional families. Their fathers were both emotionally and physically absent. Their mothers often tried to compensate for this loss. In the process, the Flying Boy learned to reject his masculinity and grew to overvalue the feminine. He experienced his feminine side vicariously through his mother and other motherlike women in his life.

I wrote this book to heal my "Flying Boy" wound and to heal my relationship with my parents and with the women I have loved. This book can also help those women who discover they have loved Flying Boys.

This is a story about feelings — losing them — finding them — and finally expressing them. Also woven throughout is a sad love song about a woman's unconditional love. All of the characters in this book are living people, and I have changed some names to protect their privacy. Laural is a composite character based on more than one woman I have loved and hurt.

You will find people you know in my story. You will learn how you may have hurt those people and been hurt by them. You will also discover a great deal of your own anger, hurt and sadness. You will see how we stuff our emotions and feelings deep inside ourselves and hold them there. We learned to believe that it was somehow superior and more spiritual to hold in our feelings, even at the cost of our health and well-being.

You will find a way out of your anger, sadness and depression and discover safe, sane ways to express yourself without fear.

This book talks about grieving, a very misunderstood process often confused with self-pity. Self-pity often leads to or perpetuates self-destruction in a variety of forms and is substantially different from grieving. Grieving is your right and is a grounding, cleansing and finally healing experience.

There is hope for Flying Boys/Wounded Men and for women who love them. Like myself, many men are healing themselves right now and thus allowing the Flying Boy's positive side to fully emerge. This book will further the healing process by helping the Flying Boy land, love and then gently labor to create peace and joy within himself, his family, society and the world. It will also open doors to understanding, compassion and empathy for women who love wounded men.

# 1 COMING TOGETHER

*Lovers don't finally meet somewhere.*
*They're in each other all along.*

Rumi

I know that the path is to be walked alone or with someone other than Laural. We met on that path. We made love, got to know each other, became friends in sadness and sanity and finally said good-bye.

Making love was easy. Getting to really know each other, becoming friends and finally saying good-bye was the hardest part.

In 1981 I moved to Austin from Alabama, where I had lived all my adult life. Two years before, I had reluctantly completed a graduate degree at the University of Alabama. I taught there for two years. I had seen the '60s and '70s come and go, leaving the South permanently scarred and changed, mostly for the better. I moved to Austin still brokenhearted

from the last two failed relationships and depressed over a life
poorly lived. Depression and myself were still my two greatest
enemies. I had to hide both from all who wanted to know me.
I hid under the masks of peacefulness, calmness and spirituality. Those who did get close saw right through my less-
than-convincing facade. No one saw more clearly than Laural.

After much debate and fantasizing about San Francisco, I
had finally chosen Austin, Texas, as my new home. I was
bored and blue in Alabama. My best friend of 15 years was
living in Texas "in sin" (as mine and his parents would still
say even in the '80s) with a wealthy woman who studied self-
help literature and theater while living on her grandfather's oil
money. She loaned me both money and a car to help get me
here so I could counsel her on how to stay with this man who
didn't have the word "stay" in his vocabulary. When I got here
I listened, though it wasn't long before he left.

Before Gene left for New Mexico, he and I agreed to meet
and have a beer at one of Austin's bar and grills. Gene and I
finally got to our table and began one of our lengthy
discussions about relationships, politics, religion and
relationships. The former and the latter topic was what we
were always talking about then, and everything else was just
filler in between talking about the one thing that everyone
was having the most trouble understanding.

Gene is a small, stocky man who is as full of integrity as he
is of ideas and information on a wide variety of subjects. His
blue eyes pierce you as effectively as his words. We love to
talk philosophically, couching everything in Alabamese.

In the middle of mouthing the words, I saw Laural for the
first time. She walked by our table without a word.

"Gene — that's the woman," I said. "If I can't be with her,
I don't want to be with anyone in Austin." The words came
out automatically as if someone else were speaking them.

"Man, you are crazy. You don't even know who that woman
is." Gene was surprised and making fun of me for my bizarre
statement.

I know exactly who that woman is. She is a lot like Susan,
the next to the last woman I had successfully run off.

It was several months before I met the woman who changed my life. I kept going to the bar and grill where she worked and watched every move she made. I saw the saddest eyes I'd ever seen. But when she walked, she moved with such grace. She wasn't very friendly to me, or to anyone else, for that matter. Something seemed to be troubling her very deeply. I had no idea that I was soon to join a long list of disappointments that had created the sadness in her eyes.

The short Austin spring had arrived. I was in the apartment that served as my stopover and shower center. It was close to the university, where I was half-heartedly working on another degree while teaching at the nearby community college.

While I was sitting on my couch, my inner voice practically yelled at me. The voice (which I know to be the strong intuition that was passed to me from my mother) said, "Get up right now and go for a run down the trail, and there you will meet the woman from the bar." (There was a nice hike and bike trail just blocks from my house.) I balked at the voice, thinking that it couldn't be right. It was after all a small trail in a large city with many small trails. But I had learned to listen to that voice, even when I doubted it.

I immediately got up, dressed and went on my run. I was still only half convinced until I ran into her not more than 15 minutes later. She stood smiling against the tall trees that lined the trail. My intuition had led me there and something greater than both of us led us to that spot in time.

Her eyes, which were greenish-brown, could hardly be looked into for the sadness that covered them like a thick fog. She presented a warm smile as an offering in the ceremony of our coming together.

We said hello, introducing ourselves. I mentioned that I had seen her in the cafe often. She said that she too had seen me. After a half-dozen more cliches, I chose to run on without her. On the way home I felt stunned and stupid for leaving her. I stopped, waiting and hoping that she'd come back the same way. I thought about how I had just failed to make anything more than superficial contact with the woman I knew I wanted to be with more than anybody I had ever known.

Not more than 10 minutes later she came running up to the spot where I was fantasizing about our future together. I spoke to her again and she willingly stopped. We talked and walked and I discovered that she only lived one block away from me.

"Would you like to come over for a beer?" she asked as we got to that crucial point in our conversation that was either leading to a "good-bye" or a real "hello".

"Sure," was all I could say. Eloquence was as distant as my composure.

We drank beer in her backyard in a swing that would later be the seat of much lovemaking and conversation. We watched the sun go down and talked about everything under it.

I learned that the way she made contact with people and things was through her art. She invited me in to view her latest work. Our painful relationship was born in that moment. In those pictures I saw the soul of the one who took them. I loved that soul for years while I learned to seek and reclaim my own.

The relationship began. From the first there was a unity that existed between us that would never be abolished by time, space, pain or anger. The days were filled with longing for each other, and the nights were spent satisfying the day's desire. I felt the hole inside me that had been dark and empty for years. The mornings were spent in more lovemaking, coffee-drinking and conversing. I showed her the image of a self that didn't really exist but wanted to. She showed me sides of herself that no one had seen or been trusted with. The movies we saw, the walks we took, the talks we had and the wide awake nights we spent all became little bridges we constructed to reach each other.

I thought I wanted more; yet now I realize how much I wanted less. I wanted her to give everything of herself to me while I only claimed to be willing to give her my all. She was more willing than I realized to give everything if I would only accept her as she was and wait as she built trust. I could not give everything because at that point I didn't have everything to give, although I talked like I did. I thought I knew all about

*When she opened*
*to me like a flower*
*but I fell on her*
*like a stone*
*I fell on her like a stone.*

"Belly Song", Etheridge Knight

love, religion and everything in between. She knew about love and spirituality and embodied both.

The arguments came like summer thunderstorms — violent and refreshing. I loved intensity in everything even if I couldn't let out my own anger. I was frustrated by the fact that Laural could.

The lovemaking was powerful because it was about the only time I could feel. At the worst of times that was all we had, and it's what kept us together. She communicated so well with her body, as I talked with my mouth, saying nothing. I quickly learned I was out of touch with my own body.

We lived in a wonderful old house near the U.T. campus. I wandered around that house like a lost child looking for hiding places from her and myself. I was always restless, waiting for one of us to leave. I had been programmed since childhood to believe that I would be left. I expected it to the point that I needed to do whatever possible to make my self-fulfilling prophecy come true. That was a way of staying in control of my life that had been so full of chaos and pain. If I could predict coming events with preciseness, I had a slim chance for survival.

She always seemed to be wondering when I would calm down and be the man I presented myself to be — spiritual, easy-going and mature. In truth my stomach seethed with unreleased anger, anxiety and tension. I had no idea who God was though I taught Religious Studies, and had read hundreds of books on religion.

I constantly criticized everything she did and nagged like no one else could. I pointed out her every personality flaw as a way to keep from facing my own. And mature? I was grandfatherly with advice and forever making decisions for her in areas that I knew nothing about.

These things were our secrets. Everyone else saw me the way I wanted them to. She saw me the way I was and loved me anyway. She was part of my secret. I did not want to share her and her knowledge of me with anyone. I hid her much like I hid myself. She knew this and was deeply angered and hurt by it.

We traveled to Arkansas early in our togetherness, on a trip

I will never forget because it signaled the beginning of the end. I saw a woman begin something I knew nothing about but would learn much about soon — grieving. She also showed me that it is absolutely necessary to grieve only with one you can trust or else alone.

We parked by a small creek. The water washed through the campsite loudly and became our 24-hour mantra. Laural and I were getting along well at this time, but her sadness was like a wall. It separated her from me and the rest of the world, and more importantly, from herself.

Evening gently approached as we made camp. The trees were green and large and no one was around us but them. We felt safe. "Laural, what's the matter?"

"I can't tell you." But her whole body asked for one thing. I held her. We sat looking at the flowing water as the tears began to flow down her cheeks. At first, tears came violently as if from some infinite source. I held her tightly. She said nothing. She crawled into my lap like a child searching for a good mother. I rocked her gently, this beautiful sad woman. And the tears she shed proved the existence of a soul, because tears like those could only come from that place. She wanted to trust me that moment. She intuitively knew that I was not ready to nurture her soul. That afternoon in the mountains she began grieving. She started and stopped there only to teach me that grieving was necessary for all of us, although she herself could not finish what she had begun.

After our trip the days were filled with fighting and arguing, whereas the nights were still being lit by candles and passion. We proceeded to a time we both knew awaited us — a time to say good-bye.

There were many things that helped to create a huge chasm between us. One was my desire to get married and immediately begin a family. I wanted a child then with such an intensity that the thought of waiting wounded me more. Our lives and our relationship was too messy and destructive to support this highest form of creativity. With much love and debate Laural decided that she could not marry me at the moment for a good reason — me. I was not ready to make a commitment to a woman or a child. She knew it — I didn't.

I needed a child because I had never really been one, having had to grow up in many ways by the time I was five. I wanted a child to carry my own lost childhood. When we finally decided not to marry and have a baby my feelings for Laural diminished. I started thinking it was time to move on and find another city, college and woman.

About a year later I decided it was time to fly away. The arguments had increased steadily in intensity and frequency. We tore at each other daily until I finally left the woman I loved almost more than God. And when I did I felt free and good for a while. I knew we had to be apart. It was not one week later that I met a woman who would in three months time help move me another step closer to reclaiming my own lost soul.

I felt it the day before it began. That morning in October was as ominous as it was clear and bright. I awoke knowing I was going to meet someone special that day. I had no idea who, but I changed shirts four times looking for the right one. Something was different because I hadn't been concerned about my attire since my early 20s when I had sold clothes for a living.

As I rode my bike to World Provision Company, where I was working part-time as a consultant, I felt elated about my newly acquired freedom from Laural. At the same moment I was anxious about the person I knew I was going to encounter.

Kim walked into my office looking for a job as desperately as I had unconsciously been looking for her. Two hours later we had talked about everything but business and had made a lunch date. Little did we know that only weeks later we would be walking through parks talking about a life together in San Francisco.

Kim was everything Laural wasn't, and everything I tried to act like I was, or wanted to be: writer, parent, prophet, and poet. She, like me, was cold, out of touch with her body and feelings and talked much more than touched. We both lived in our heads to escape pain and any possibility of intimacy and commitment while we searched the world of fantasy and dreams looking for our souls and our soulmates.

I thought she was mine. I thought I loved her, and in truth what happened, as I wandered up in the air with this attractive golden-haired woman who looked like my mother, is that I found the mirror that I had been looking for since childhood. My mother had not been the mirror I needed and longed for. Kim was, whereas Laural only was to a degree. Kim showed me to me. She and I were so much alike it was frightening and enlightening.

I looked into her face and saw my own. Her lines and creases were mine. Her despair and disappointments were mine. Her darkness echoed my own. Her dramas I had staged a thousand times. As narcissistic as this may sound it is absolutely necessary that at some point, hopefully in childhood, we find a mirror.

Sadly, I was my mother's mirror. I reflected her own image but I could not see myself in her face. I could see how her face lit up when I would be a good boy and be what she needed me to be — her confidant, savior and saint. I spent most of my life trying to light up the faces of the mothers I met, always afraid that they would not be pleased if I was just myself.

It was through Kim that I made partial contact with myself. I had been preparing to do so for 10 years, having read everything I could find that C.G. Jung had said about the anima or feminine soul that all men have. They usually project it onto physical, external women rather than recognize it in themselves. The contact was powerful. At that moment I began to reclaim my feminine soul and also to rediscover my own true but negated masculinity. I began to love myself when I began loving her, after having lived so long with the belief that I was ultimately unlovable since I was so full of self-doubt and hatred.

As I accepted Kim, I began the process of accepting myself. As I made love to her I was making love to me. And as I did, something from very deep in my unconscious began struggling to surface like a diver whose air hose has been cut. There was a deep sadness and sorrow waiting to emerge. My dreams were filled with images and messages that told me a great unity needed to happen.

Kim and I were together for three months. I was different.

I was aware of the necessity of the change that was coming. When she finally left I entered the second deepest depression I had ever experienced. But I had a knowledge of something I could not explain. Laural felt pain from my being with this person that she would never quite forget. Kim left; the dreams and the changes kept coming; the depression began to lift, and Laural reluctantly came back.

Laural and I attempted to be friends during my brief, tempestuous romance with Kim. Laural despised these attempts. Kim and I parted after a fiery trip to Jamaica, where we learned that a beach and one too many glasses of wine do not make up for premature plans. While roaming the beach alone for hours, I realized that I missed Laural more than I could say. I tried to relay my feelings to her in a letter. This was consistent with every trip I ever took alone when we were living together. Every time I left to taste temporary freedom it was bitter while the taste of her lingered. Whenever I got where I was going, I would long to have her there by me.

I was always leaving, flying away from women, jobs, commitments and myself. No matter who the woman was, I was as good as gone the moment we made love. It was at that moment that I always touched something taboo — perhaps my mother, perhaps my pain — and I would have to fly away. The woman with me might think our relationship wonderful. Yet I worried and waited for the most appropriate moment to take flight. If I didn't fly away I ran them off. Either way I knew that I couldn't be with them.

I lived in a beautiful home in Hyde Park with a pet and a friend. Kim, who was no longer speaking to me, lived only two blocks away. Kim and I had parted with much destruction and depression. I sliced her with great verbal swords that wounded her deeply the day after dreaming that she had slept with the man who nearly destroyed her prior to our coming together. She had. I told her everything bad about herself. It only took a couple of hours to reduce her to one gigantic tear. I stripped her of every mask I had ever worn. It would be weeks before I would fully realize what I had done. My transformation had advanced one step further, but at the high cost of disfiguring the image one woman had of herself and thus leaving another casualty in the wake of my painful growth.

Laural came to my house several days after Kim and I returned from Jamaica. She was still angry with me for rejecting her in the cruel way I had. It was a sunny Saturday afternoon. She had just gotten off work and came by for what was to be a brief visit. We sat in the backyard and talked about our love for each other, how I had hurt her deeply, and the possibility of our getting back together to try one more time.

We made a decision while she sat on the picnic table looking at me the way she did during the first months of our togetherness. The passion of those early months appeared like a welcome guest that we carried to bed.

We were together again, but this time something very different was happening inside me. During the trip with Kim to Jamaica something had begun to happen. I did not know what, and I was more than a little afraid of what I heard and saw. The first sign was in our lovemaking. When I had an orgasm, a deep, disturbing moan such as I had never heard or made before came out of me. It was frightening because I knew the depths from which it came. I was like a wounded animal making a death cry to its mate. It scared Kim and me. It would consistently recur for two years before it ended.

I was beginning to act differently by being more assertive. This was totally unlike the me who was always trying to say the right thing and to please anyone who needed pleasing — for instance, in Montego Bay, when Kim and I were running late for our flight home. The taxi driver was dawdling, unnecessarily engaged in a leisurely chat with a friend at the hotel desk. With only minutes to spare, I walked up to him, slapped my hand on the desk and stated my case and my needs. Moments later we were being whisked to the airport, and I knew something had just happened that was positive and masculine. I was ready for more and to explore the possibilities that more did not necessarily mean macho.

# 2 TOUCHING THE WOUND

*Big boys aren't supposed to cry.*

My father

Laural started seeing me again. I changed a little and was depressed a lot. The changes that occurred for another two years began the moment that Kim left and would increase significantly after Laural left me a year later. Those years were packed with pain, grief, sadness and anger.

Shortly after Kim left I had the most incredible dreams. In a dark barn I met a small mouse and a hawk that had exactly the same color and identical markings. I was issued the task by something inside myself to simultaneously befriend the mouse and the hawk — the timid and the assertive — the prey and the predator. When I awoke that morning and recorded my dream, I felt the need for the two natures to be reconciled. The dream was a powerful sign from my soul. But the dream included no information about how this was to be done.

13

Several nights later in a dream I was subtly shown the way
to unite the hawk and the mouse. It came with such
emotional impact and clarity that I was forced to consider its
implications for years to come. In this dream, I was lying in
bed in my new Hyde Park house. Someone entered my
bedroom and told me my father had died. I was saddened
beyond words. I walked out of the house into my backyard,
threw my head back and howled at the dark sky like a
wounded wolf, but only one time. I immediately stopped for
fear that I might awaken the elderly man next door. I walked
back into the house, repressing my remorse. There a group
of men were convened to mourn the death of my father. Yet
I could not show any emotion or feeling.

I knew finally and alarmingly, after having worked in
therapy for years on the issues that surrounded my relationship to my mother, that it was time to work on my sadness
and anger about my father. I had not seen him in several
years and had never really communicated with him in my
life. I denied this fact for years though I had been dreaming
of my father on the average of three to five nights a week for
as long as I could remember. The dreams were always filled
with violence, rage, anger and hatred. The pain of the wound
I received from him was too great and disturbing to
remember and bring into the light of consciousness for
examination or reflection. But then I knew I must if I was
going to heal myself.

Months earlier, Bly had told me how necessary it was for
men to do this, but I did not want to listen. Now I was ready.
I began.


Slowly and painfully I began getting in touch with the rage
and grief I felt toward my alcoholic, abusive father who was
never around when I needed him. Even though I had
convinced myself that he didn't matter to me, I hated him. I
tried to do everything just the opposite of the way he had,
and tried as hard as I could to never be like him. The truth
was, in many ways, we were one and the same. Whenever
someone pointed this out to me — usually a girlfriend or my
sister — I hated it.

Getting in touch with my feelings about my father began with the dreams. This was facilitated by a visit to an incredible healer named Rachel Clair. She began to put me in touch with a nice but ignored body that had been taking my head from place to place.

Rachel is a small, red-haired woman with a timeless face. She has been a student of the body/mind/soul for more than 25 years. She has learned more than a dozen theories and techniques for helping people rediscover and remember that they are the body they have forgotten and often abused for so long.

I made an appointment with Rachel and, unknowingly, a rendezvous with myself. Those two hours were unforgettable. I made the first of many connections to come with my own body and its pain. I, like many others, had shut down and disconnected from that part of me to save another part. The pain, discomfort and rejection I felt as a child was housed in my body/mind, and therefore I felt I had to flee it and leave it behind. I shut down my feeling self and flew up into my mind. I thought I was safe there, and in trying to think everything out gave myself and others headaches in the process. I educated my mind and forgot I had a body except in extreme circumstances — either sexual or suicidal. I stored as much information as possible in my cerebral silo. It was full of facts, fiction and fantasy. And I was an educated failure. I felt nothing — certainly neither love nor peace.

My body was just as full of pain and memories. What was in me began coming out on that table in Rachel's office. She massaged, balanced, rebirthed, acupressured and reconnected me by touching the temple that I had all but forgotten and left unvisited. I wept and shouted in agony from the same depths as the orgasms I'd had with Kim and then with Laural. A great sadness had set in, and a new energy was rising as I began feeling my body after more than 25 years of neglect.

Through her techniques she showed me that while I was able to own some of the pain stored on my left side (which in Eastern thought is considered the feminine side), I could not even comprehend the incredible pain that was coming from my right side. When she worked on my left side I would lean my head in that direction and moan or cry. When she touched the right side, I automatically gritted my teeth, threw my head back away from my body, and did not make a sound. John Wayne and Dad would have been so proud of me since, after all, "big boys aren't supposed to cry". But when I got off that table, something wonderful and different had happened inside me that no one could take away or deny.

A couple of days after my session with Rachel, I realized a new energy was rising and making itself known for the first time: a masculine energy that at first would be very unfamiliar and uncomfortable. I began noticing my body more — not in a narcissistic way, but rather feeling the little pains, the soreness and the stress. A sadness started to rise at the recognition that I had not noticed my body since childhood. I was also beginning to feel anger at the fact that I hadn't really ever felt my body except in extreme circumstances. Anger was surfacing. This was very scary and very necessary.

One afternoon while walking to my office at U.T., Kim and I ran into each other by accident or fate. Still angry at me, she began accosting me there on the street. In my usual "counselorish" manner I listened and tried to figure out a way to take this verbal abuse without getting angry myself, because I thought she had a right to her anger, although I didn't have a right to mine. Suddenly I had had enough, and out of my mouth popped words that expressed this in an angry, assertive, but thoroughly appropriate manner.

"Kim," I said, "I'm sorry I said those things to you (I had already apologized once before). I was wrong. Forgive me. But enough is enough. I'm not going to stand here and take this abuse!"

I turned and walked away. I was amazed. That was the first time I could recall being angry without my anger imme- diately turning into tears. It was wonderful. After years of being afraid to be angry, I finally could be. In my family, anger equaled pain, rejection or violence. When Dad was angry, which he always was, someone would dearly pay — usually me, my mother or my sister. Dad would yell and scream — mother would get a migraine and I would have to take care of her. I might get a whipping (a euphemism for beating) or my sister and I might get sent to our room. But it was clear that anger hurt. Anger became deeply associated with pain in my mind and my body.

I could not understand and would not be comfortable with anger for at least two more years of hard work and repeated failure to express it appropriately. I had so much anger in me that had not been expressed. Laural, like other people, could not deal with my anger because it was bigger than both of us. When I got angry about one thing and tried to tell her about it, it was impossible. That one event became a release mechanism for years of stored up anger at my father, mother, first girlfriend, or whomever or whatever I did not get angry at sometime in the past. My unreleased anger was partially responsible for my inability to communicate.

During this time I observed Laural closely. Before my experiences with Rachel and Kim, when Laural had become angry, I was terrified.

"Laural," I'd say, "stop yelling at me! Don't yell at me! Calm down! If you don't stop, I'm leaving." In essence what I demanded was that she swallow her anger as I had mine.

With wonder and awe I'd watch Laural. She'd get angry, scream, throw things and then it would be over — no migraines — no whippings — no more anger. And all the while I rationalized that I was spiritually more together than her since I "never got angry". I was beginning to see that expressed anger was healthy and what I had been doing was making me sicker and sicker. But I wasn't quite ready for the cure. I kept storing and stuffing.

The depression steadily deepened. The number of pleasant times Laural and I had as a couple decreased. We were together, but not really. We made love but there was no longer life in it. I wore her down and tore down her self-image as I looked outward for answers to the questions I had been asking of religion, psychology and philosophy for years. I kept looking in Laural's face for my feminine soul. Laural wanted to be loved and liked for who and what she was, but definitely not the repository for my wandering, missing soul.

*Nobody can counsel and help you, nobody.*
*There is only one single way.*
*Go into yourself.*

Rilke

I did not see this for years though I knew it intellectually.

I entered psychotherapy once again. This time I saw an eclectic Freudian woman, after having tried a Humanistic and a Jungian therapist, both who had primed me for this last analyst. Dr. Mary Mason and I worked together for two years. She became a major factor in my forming a future that at the time I couldn't even fantasize.

The darkness was beginning to engulf both Laural and me. Laural could see the consequences. I couldn't — I was so accustomed to the dark I thought it only natural and even noble. She thought it was destructive. She kept telling me our relationship wasn't working — I kept telling her the reason was because she didn't love me enough.

"Laural, if you'd just open up and let me in — trust me, really trust me. You just don't love me. You really don't know what love is." I must have said these words to her a thousand times in two years.

"I do love you; I am open to you but it takes time to build trust. You don't just turn everything loose overnight. It takes time." She'd say this over and over again but I wouldn't hear. After all it was I who had read all the books and great poems about love.

"Bullshit! If you really loved me you'd be open and be trusting right now . . . this minute."

I was unable to see she loved me. I refused to see. Seeing meant staying. Staying meant feeling. I couldn't feel and I couldn't stay or commit to anything or anybody.

Thanks to Jung, Bly, Rachel, James Hillman and most of all Laural, I began to understand that I was worst at feeling. I was much better at thinking. But I could fool my fellow nonfeelers. They labeled me as sensitive, gentle, a great feeler. I could talk about feeling and how badly we should feel about the poor, the hungry and the oppressed.

And then Laural would say, "John, will you just hold me?" I could not respond with any feeling at all except perhaps anger at her ability to ask for what she needed and my inability to give it.

"I can't right now — I'm busy." "What, you want to make love again? I'm tired." "I'm watching TV." "I'm depressed."

What I was really saying was, "Sorry, can't feel a thing from my head down to my toes."

Laural could feel and she could communicate her feelings with her body and she enjoyed it. I, in my pseudo-spirituality, considered her decadent, and yet her sensuality at times saved us. It would be years before I'd fully realize her abilities and her love.

It would take her leaving to show me the truth of myself. She loved me and herself enough to remove herself from a destructive situation. She left because it wasn't working and it hadn't worked for a long time. We weren't friends — we were just fellow sufferers who survived the lovemaking ceremonies we created to try to heal each other and especially me.

By the time she left I had stripped her psyche. Her self-confidence was shaky at best anyway. I wounded her spirit with my darkness and dire incompleteness. I projected onto her my faults, flaws and soul, and tried to force her to carry them. She finally refused to participate in such madness and cruelty and left. In the next year and a half I'd see — her love — her — myself.

The days were almost unbearable. The vacuum that had always existed increased tenfold. The pain of her going was greater than I had anticipated. The emptiness swallowed me, and it felt like pieces of me were scattered all over Austin. I was convinced she carried a large piece of me with her wherever she went. I tried everything to get her and that missing piece back. Nothing worked.

One week after she left I was taking an early morning walk down the street I lived on and saw her parked car. The same one we had bought, traveled in and fought in. It was parked on the street in front of a house then unknown to me. It was 7 a.m.; I walked a half a block further and felt a kind of pain I hadn't known in years from a place I didn't know existed. Not able to walk any farther I sat on the curb and cried and, as the sun came up, I went deeper down into myself.

Several days later I went to Laural with suicidal thoughts such as I had never before experienced. I told her how her leaving was affecting me. She listened as I told her how much

I hurt and how unfair it was of her to leave me this way. Not only had she left, but she was already with another man.

"How can you show so little respect for what we had?" I asked. "And for yourself? You're already involved with someone and our relationship hasn't even had time to cool down. Don't you see you're just using him to help you get out of a difficult situation because you don't have the strength to do it on your own? Goddamn you — I hate you for what you're doing to us."

"This relationship hasn't ever worked and you know it. We need to let it go." She looked like she wanted to cry but didn't. "This man is what I need right now. I still love you and care about what happens to you, but I can't be with you anymore." Her words would be repeated for almost two years, and each time I would cry, rage and wonder if they were really true.

She was too sympathetic at times, and she never let me forget that she knew what I was going through because it was so similar to her feelings when I was with Kim. She was trying to be the friend I said I could be but really couldn't when I was with Kim.

The pain turned into a sickness that was to signal that the sanity and soul I had long ago lost were soon to be recovered. But before that could happen, thoughts of suicide had to be delved into, and much, much more had to happen.

I became very ill. My stomach began cramping profusely in a way that was frightening. I took to my bed for more than two weeks the first time and then about 18 days the second time. The sweat and the chills were counterpoints. I couldn't eat, excrete or die. As I lay there, thoughts ran through my mind like tortured demons. My temperature increased to 104 degrees as the fires of memory raged and consumed my strength and energy.

I'd call Laural — she'd come over and stay a while and then leave to go home to her new lover. Depression covered me like the blankets I was sweating into. Thoughts of suicide began flickering across my mind like a slow, silent film.

I began visiting doctors with hopes for some medical cure for my spiritual and psychological condition. The diagnosis, was stress — the modern answer for a modern problem. This was not good enough nor dramatic enough for me. Finally one doctor prematurely diagnosed what I had as cancer of the stomach. Now there was a disease worth my time and death. That should get Laural back, I thought. But the tests said no, I didn't have the modern plague.

Finally, out of frustration with the medical establishment, I diagnosed my own case. My diagnosis was neither banal nor dramatic, but as accurate as they get. I was sick to my stomach with my life, like my mother had been with hers; and I couldn't help but see how she used illness to cope and to solicit support from me, as a temporary reprieve from the world and my father. But the sickness with life — my life, could only be cured if I could change my life. I didn't know how right at the moment of diagnosis, so my prognosis was not very hopeful. I got more depressed. My stomach had always been a problem and a connector to my mother. It was now full of pain that served as a primer to be used to pump out the poisonous anger and sadness that accumulated for nearly three decades.

I struggled to free myself from my mother's sickbed and the depression that held me there. I unconsciously wrote my own prescription based on the information and the insights I had gathered over the years and while lying there on my back. I had to go deeper into the causes of the pain and the depression even though I was weak, afraid and alone — or so I thought.

I felt I was losing my mind and my partial hold on reality. I had hidden in my mind while my stomach shouted that I had better "come out, come out, wherever I was". I hid there for good reasons. As a child I was a "feeler" but had too many painful encounters with an angry father and an overly dependent mother. I gave up feeling for thinking. Luckily I kept my intuitive tendencies intact. Dad, due in part to alcohol and part to anger, was not exactly the ideal father. Rather, he was like many men of the '40s and '50s. He simply was not at home much. He was absent from my life and my mother's life. When he was there he offered us little. He was tired from working in a factory for 40 slow hours each week.

When at home he was either high from aclohol or low from too much television. Either way he was remote and removed from what was going on with me.

My mother was alone much of the time. When I was there, she turned a lot of her attention and energy toward me. This worked out fine because I was starved for attention and love. What I did not know then was that I needed both masculine and feminine affection, values and energy. She compensated for Dad's tendency to reject and ridicule me with his perfectionist attitude and angry demeanor. She also tried to compensate for her own unhappiness by making me into a surrogate husband and her own little armored knight and protector.

My mother's tendency to use me to get what she was not getting from her husband made my father unconsciously even harder on me. He was jealous, which later would hurt both of us. Dad and Mom fought a lot about everything, mostly money, bills and his drinking. She developed illnesses galore as a coping mechanism early in her own childhood, as she had been a child in an alcoholic home herself. Sickness got her some attention. Dad would yell and get drunk and she'd get sick. She had migraine after migraine as well as stomach problems, and she'd call for her sedatives — me, aspirin and, later, Valium.

For a while I felt my own pain, but quickly exchanged it for hers after realizing my own was too much for either of us to deal with. I shut down my feeling side and began thinking about how I could make the world a better place for Mom and others. It looked like my own life was doomed to destruction and frustration. In the process, I began stuffing my feelings and emotions into my stomach and thinking of ways to survive. Ironically, this only gave me the same migraines mother endured. I lost touch with the body that was beaten and abused and a house full of painful memories.

I grew up in what clinicians call a dysfunctional family — boy was it ever! My world was perceived as hostile and chaotic, and the people in it were untrustworthy. I would not — could not — dared not trust anyone. If you can't trust your parents, who can you trust?

There was something sad and sinister about a particular afternoon that made it seem like a waking nightmare. The pain in me seemed to be reflected in everything I saw. The stomach illness had loosened its grip though the depression had not. Laural came by for one of her short "I can't stay too long" visits. I kept forgetting we weren't in love anymore because I still was. This day she would end up staying much longer than planned.

Laural and I sat for a while in her car. We slid open the side door to watch the sun set. We talked about our past relationship and present pain. She was willing to listen but I still wasn't saying anything.

I never really communicated my feelings to her very well, though I was considered by my students and colleagues to be eloquent and well-equipped to explain even complicated things so that anyone could understand. I took great pride in this ability. Yet when it came to telling the ones I loved the most what I really felt, it was as if I were dumb. There was so much pain and fear separating me from my feelings that all I could do was talk about things from an intellectual standpoint. I couldn't get through to her or to my feelings.

This inability to communicate began in childhood. I was never able to tell my father how I felt. I was scared of ridicule and rejection. I swallowed my feelings or modified them and took them to my mother, even though it wasn't the same. With her I had to hide my true self for fear that if she found out who I really was, not nearly as strong as I felt she needed me to be, would be as disappointed in me as it seemed my father was. I couldn't take rejection from both, so that I hid or edited my statements to everyone, never expressing the anger or the hurt I felt. In time I learned to hide behind words, ideas, concepts and jargon. I was safe but sorry to be stuck in my mind.

It took me another year or so to connect my inability to talk to Laural with my inability to talk to my father. They are so much alike in many ways. I knew that I was attracted to certain women because they reminded me of my mother. Laural certainly did with her fragile looks, long blonde hair and sad eyes. What I did not know was that she was more like my

*When the evening is spread out against the sky
Like a patient etherised upon a table . . .*

T. S. Eliot

father than I ever would have guessed. Laural was often distant, cold and withdrawn just as Dad had been all during my life. It took a while for me to realize that by being with her I not only continued my mother complex but I also had the opportunity to work on unfinished business with my father. If I got Laural's approval and affection, I was vicariously getting the love of the father I never knew and thought I hated.

We sat in the car not really communicating but unconsciously preparing for what would come next. "John, why don't you let it out?" Laural asked as she held my hand and looked deeply at the "It" in me that she had seen from the very beginning.

"What do you mean?"

"I mean let out what's inside you — the hurt, the pain, the sadness and the anger you feel."

I felt Laural's support. I knew she understood how much was in me that desperately needed to be released. But I couldn't trust anyone. People could tell me anything. I would listen and care but I seldom shared even small parts of myself with anyone — not even my therapists, let alone the people I loved the most. I feared they would abandon me if they knew I was something other than what I pretended to be.

"Laural — I can't. I just can't," I just kept repeating. "If I did, I don't know what would happen. I might go mad. Besides there's no one that can be with me. If I said what was really inside they would have to leave. Look, you've left." The tension built in my shoulders and my throat was getting tighter and more constricted.

"John, I have seen it; that's why I had to leave." Laural held my hand as she spoke. "You were killing me with your repressed emotions — not because they existed, but because you refused to let them out. You've kept everything in so long it's turned into poison that has destroyed you and everyone who wants to love you."

"I can't." A tear fell. "You're with another man. I need you. I just can't."

Control. I couldn't let go because I had to be in control of my emotions. I had to be in control of my world and, whenever possible, other people's worlds as well. I had tried to control Laural through manipulation, education and domination while paying lip service to feminism and equality. I always had to be in control. I could never be late. I couldn't stand to be kept waiting — control in a hundred different ways. If I could just control or maintain the illusion of control by predicting and programming my existence and environment, I thought I might just have a chance in this world. This came from having to second guess the needs and moods of my parents. They were both so unpredictable; my mother's head could ache or my father's alcoholic temper could flare and hurt me or my sister.

After an hour or so we finally moved from the car to the front lawn. I brushed myself off as I tried to brush off the feelings that were rising to the surface and wanting to come out like little demons that I dared not disturb.

Once in the house, that was as dark and dreary as I was, we sat together on my couch. The sun was gone and the darkness wrapped me as tightly as Laural did with her arms. I fell into those arms like they were a safety net waiting for my descent. I kept falling. "John, let it out!" she gently said as she held me lightly.

"Laural, I can't. I just can't. I hurt too much and there's too much in there. If I ever started I'm afraid I'd never stop."

"John, trust me. You have to trust and let go. I can't come back to you, but I won't leave you. I'll be there for you. Trust me."

Tears started to fall and she held me even tighter as they did. I stopped and pulled out of her arms. "Laural, I just can't," my voice cracked.

"Yes, you can — you have to. It's right."

Finally I began crying again from deep inside the place where the hurt child lives. I started heaving and sobbing from that place where adult prisoners live who have been sentenced for life without knowledge of their crimes. I cried and stopped — cried and stopped. I was so afraid of where I was going, what I was doing and who I was doing it with. This was the woman who had left me. Should I go into the desert and die? Would I still love Laural? Would I still be a good teacher or even be able to teach? Or would I just go down the main street of town babbling and begging? I didn't know.

"Laural," I sputtered, "I've never trusted anyone in my whole goddamn miserable life — not my parents, not my best friends and certainly not you. How can I trust? And yet I know I need to trust someone so badly. But I've always believed a person will one day leave. Don't you see? My own parents couldn't be trusted, and in a way they left me a long time ago. If they'll leave, anybody will."

Laural listened and held me tighter with each tear that fell. And finally, with a great heave, I began. And she rocked me and stroked my head. The grieving began that evening.

I began yelling, "I hurt so much. I hurt so much. It hurt me that you left. It hurt me so much that we couldn't have the family I wanted so much. I wanted so much to be the man I pretended to be and that you asked God to send you. I hurt so much. I haven't seen my father in four years. I feel so much pain and I hurt because my father never spent time with me and my mother spent too much. I hate him so much and love him so much. I hurt for hurting you so much. I just couldn't help it. I hurt when my parents put me on that Goddamn 24-hour bus ride when I was six. I was alone. It hurt to see my father drunk and hurting my mother and beating me and my sister until our legs bled. God I hurt!"

Things like this came up for four hours — memories, pain, sadness, anger and rage. I kept crying and she kept holding me. She didn't run away. She wasn't afraid. She didn't offer advice. She just listened as I dipped out tears and pain from my stagnant well of grief, not knowing what would be at the bottom.

When I stopped crying that evening I was exhausted, refreshed, saddened and stronger. I knew something miraculous had just happened inside me and between Laural and me.

As Laural got ready to leave, she sat for a few minutes in her car just looking at me as I stood a full six feet tall and six feet from her. As I stood silently before her, I saw what appeared to be a white light that surrounded her whole

being, especially around her head. In those eternal moments
I saw the person — Laural — the spirit — the body.

We were both completely revealed to one another that
evening. I saw her. I saw her as she was, and what I saw and
felt I would never forget. I felt deeply in love with the person,
not the projection, not the persona, not my anima. And I began
a journey into grief that would last a full nine months and then
for another year in a less dramatic way. We united that night
and gave birth to something — I believe and feel it was me.

# 3 THE GRIEVING BEGINS

*Grief is the doorway to a man's feelings.*

Robert Bly

The next day Laural called me on the phone, something she rarely did. "John," she said, "I had to tell you how much last night meant to me and what I saw. As I was leaving there was this beautiful white light that surrounded your whole body. I felt like I really saw you."

I told her that I too had seen the same light around her. Even so, the whole day was spent in tears, as were many following days. For nine months, with the possible exception of six to eight days, I started every day and ended each day with tears that came not from just my eyes but my whole body. I'd wake up in the middle of the night sweating, swearing, praying and crying.

I was grieving. Grieving is something very different from self-pity. Self-pity is useless and grieving is healing. I had been full of self-pity for years. But now I was grieving as if

over someone who was dying. And I was mourning the
passing of a self that no longer cared to live.

In the mornings, after a tearful beginning I would get
dressed and go teach my classes. At times I wanted to leave
the room because of the sadness that would well up inside
me. I felt like I was coming apart at the seams. Interestingly
enough though, when I received my evaluations at the end of
the semester, I found out that my students felt my perfor-
mance in class had been unusually effective and more
human.

In the evenings I would often drive around the Texas hill
country crying or take walks down by Town Lake crying and
not caring who saw me or what they thought.

Laural saw the tears and the tear that ran through my soul.
I'd call her and she'd come over when she could and stay as
long as possible. It tore her up to see me in such pain.

I began drinking quite heavily at this time and one night
was finally thrown into jail for D.W.I. The drinking and
driving ceased, but the drinking and sitting and walking
continued. No one could believe that I had let myself get out
of control to the point of possibly hurting someone in a
physical way. But I did. The saint had sunk.

It seemed like I lived on Tequila, wine, coffee and cheese
Danishes. I lost weight and sleep. Tears kept coming —
memories kept coming — awareness of my body kept
coming — and so did Laural. I knew I was going somewhere,
where I didn't know, but it felt insane.

"When is this going to stop?" I'd ask Dr. Mary Mason at
some point in every therapy session.

"It will stop when you're finished. I don't know what day
or month, but it will stop," she'd say.

It didn't stop soon enough for me, but something very new
to me was beginning to happen. I watched the tears at times
subside and give way to anger.

When I wasn't sitting half-catatonic, walking, weeping,
staring at the phone wondering what I could say to get Laural
back or praying that it would be her when it would ring, I was
exploring a new feeling.

One afternoon in the middle of my madness I was sitting in my living room floor just after another cry. It was raining and the sky was as dark as my demeanor. I started thinking about Laural being only blocks away and probably in bed with a man I didn't know but was sure I would hate. I watched the anger rise in me like an oil well ready to explode. I decided I was going to walk those few blocks, kick in the son-of-a-bitch's door and destroy him, her and his dog.

I could hardly believe what I was feeling — such rage — which I had never felt before. Rage was inside me, a devout pacifist and promoter of nonviolence during the '60s and '70s! But I was so angry I couldn't contain it and for the first time wasn't afraid to release it. When my father got angry, somebody got hit, and here I was feeling like my father whom I had always tried to forget but never tried to forgive. I was drinking like him, and now I was almost ready to be physically violent like he had been.

Then it struck me that if I went down there and hit Laural's boyfriend, I would probably get hit back, and the guy might even kill me. Nor did I want to be like Dad. I had all this anger and rage that I didn't know how to deal with, when suddenly I spied a wooden chair by my desk. All of a sudden I grabbed that chair and beat it into the floor. It folded and splintered into a thousand pieces, like myself. I kept beating it against the floor until it was nothing but a pile of kindling. I fell to my knees before it as if it were my first altar to anger. I did not know what had happened, but knew I no longer wanted to go to Steve's house and somehow I felt a little stronger. Though I was scared by my own destructive abilities, for the first time I was not being self-destructive. I had done something totally out of character and it worked. My arms felt relaxed; my breathing was full and deep, and my chest did not ache. I had not hurt anybody, including myself.

I kept working, hurting, writing and waiting in between crying and yelling into the face of God. The depression that I had been experiencing increased, and it seemed like the devil had swallowed me.

On the advice of Dr. Mary Mason, I began with another psychiatrist to further help me wrestle with my demons. He gave me encouragement and small doses of Valium to help me sleep, and then more later to temporarily ease the gloom. I was in favor of neither drugs nor encouragement, having seen my mother and aunts abuse both; but I had come to the point that my walking and waking was going to have to be turned into sleep if I was going to continue probing into the causes and possible cures of my malaise.

I was working on a doctorate at the time. I didn't believe in it or feel that I really wanted it, but thought that I needed it in order to validate myself and prove that I was as smart as anyone. I also felt that I needed to prove something to my father. I was holding down a full teaching assistantship at the University of Texas and teaching three courses a semester at the nearby community college. I worked to keep myself from seeing myself. I lost myself in my work just as my father had done. I was also counseling a few clients a week. It looked good on paper and to my peers, who could only manage half as much but were for the most part twice as sane and healthy as I. Here I was angry at a father for doing exactly the same things I was doing. I was beginning to understand him a little bit.

I kept working, and finally one day during a lecture, as I walked from one side of the room to the other, I noticed that I just didn't feel like I could make it to the other side. I felt that if I took one more step, I would collapse. I sat down on the stool I seldom used, talked for a few more minutes and then made my way to the phone.

"Dr. Mason," I said weakly, "This is John. I can't do it anymore. I can't keep up this pace. I'm falling apart. I don't know what to do. I haven't slept . . ." I began crying.

"You need a rest," she said. "We've discussed the possibility of your checking into the hospital and taking some time off. Do you feel you want to do this now?" There was a long pause and the word yes was all I could manage.

I checked into the university hospital for several days. I carried bedclothes and a copy of Saint-Exupery's *Little Prince.* I lay there—eating, watching television, sleeping and reading the *Little Prince.* I returned for a time to childhood, a land where work is for grown-ups and food was served to me like I was royalty. I ate everything in sight and rested. My strength

*It is only with the heart that one can see rightly;
what is essential is invisible to the eye.*

Saint-Exupery

and resolve slowly returned. I swallowed my pills and my pride and got ready to go back out and face those things that waited. Now I felt a commitment to take one thing at a time and be just a bit easier on myself.

One of the first things I did for myself after my hospitalization was to allow myself to become slightly, sanely involved with Barbara. She had been a former student of mine. She was blonde and bright and she reminded me of Laural in more ways that I could count. She was willing to accept my craziness temporarily since she held no designs on the future. She and I got to know each other, and I fell into her arms and felt a passion rise that I was sure had disappeared with Laural's leaving. It hadn't, but neither really had Laural.

The very next day after Barbara and I had been together, Laural called and asked if I was sleeping with someone. Laural had sensed this another time, a month before, when I had been with another woman on a one-night stand. During the moments that I was making love to that woman I was thinking and longing for Laural. I fantasized that this person was she, and that it was her lying with me. Just as I was ready to descend deeper into my fantasy, the phone rang. I felt I had to answer it.

"John, I need to talk to you. I know it's late and you can say no. But I feel I need to talk." Laural seldom said those words. I got up, apologized and drove to Laural's, leaving Rebecca frustrated, bewildered and alone in my bed. Now Laural was calling again. At least this time she waited until we and the sun were up.

"Yes, Laural, I'm seeing someone." It felt so good to say this to her. I also knew it was helping me to be with someone. What I didn't know until later was that being with Barbara was still just a more subtle way of staying connected to Laural. Even though I liked Barbara a lot, I really am sad to say that the main reason I was with her was because she was so much like Laural. And yet that's what I needed at the time.

Meanwhile, Laural and I were getting together once a week (mostly at my insistence or through our strong intuitions about where the other would be) for talks — long talks where we'd say mostly the same things over and over and usually only end up hurting each other. I still couldn't say what I really felt.

Sometimes her love and compassion for me would allow her to say yes to questions and needs when a no would have been more appropriate. One time she said yes and I stayed awake all night long and just smelled her long beautiful hair. She was indulging a sad man's need for closeness.

Once after we had spent the afternoon together walking down by Town Lake, we stopped and read to each other from a wonderful book called *She,* by Robert Johnson, in which he recounts the myths of Psyche and Aphrodite. Something happened as we sat on a bench looking out over the lake and watching a man work his three or four fishing lines — a distinct shift in my and Laural's energies and the way we related and interacted with each other occurred. I felt this shift, and though I couldn't explain logically what had happened, something important did happen.

That night I had a dream. In the dream in a psychological and spiritual way I made love to Laural as a woman makes love to a man, and Laural made love to me as only a man makes love to a woman. I felt from my head to my toes my feminine self totally take over as I became tender and could touch my lover in ways I had never been able to before. I felt what it was like to be a woman. The lovemaking was unusual and erotic as I touched my femininity and she made deep contact with her own masculinity and her own Aphrodite nature in a way that would heal her and help to further unite us, and yet simultaneously establish us as separate persons. I'll never forget that dream — that kind of lovemaking.

More anger came. The first person to receive the anger that I had been storing up for three decades was my mother. I realized how angry I was at my mother for unconsciously conspiring to usurp my masculinity, at myself for just as unknowingly giving it up and at my father for being such a poor example of masculinity.

Mothers are often the safest people to get angry at. No matter what you say, the chances are good that they will forgive and forget. In therapy men and women more readily begin working on their issues with the safest parent. I knew my mother was a major source of a lot of grief and in part responsible for the impossible relationships I formed. My mother was also partly responsible for my wonderful ability to be friends with women as long as they were just friends. But clearly the two categories existed.

Laural had been my lover. All other women were my friends. Laural hated falling into the former category and cringed each time I would introduce her to a member of the latter. She would get especially angry when a friend would tell her how lucky she must feel to be with such a gentle, understanding and compassionate man who understood the feminine side of life so well. She hated to hear this. It was as if my women friends were speaking of another person.

My mother tried to use me to heal her own wounds. We began talking about her pain in great detail by the time I was four. One day she and Dad got into one of their big arguments and Mom took to her sick bed with her migraine. "Don't worry, Mom," I said, as I soothed her brow with cool cloths and water, "I'll always take care of you."

"You're a good boy, Son," she replied. "I know I can always depend on you." And she could until now.

One day during my dark time she called and began, "Son, I'm not doing too well. My legs are giving me trouble and my heart's not good." She started giving me play by play details of her life game, a game she was obviously losing.

"Mom," I said, "I don't want to hear it. I'm coming apart at the seams and I just don't want to hear it anymore." I started crying.

"I've listened to you and listened to you complain about your life since I was a kid. What about my life, damn it?" The tears stopped and my voice went even deeper. "You and Dad made me grow up so fast when both of you refused to. I'm sick and tired of hearing about you and your sisters and how bad everything is. I don't want to hear anything from you for a while until something in each of us changes. Listen to me now. I don't want you to call and I'm not going to for a while until I get things worked out."

I paused and finally said, "I don't need your pain right now. Do you understand? No more."

My mother was devastated. I couldn't believe what I'd just said to the person who had raised me almost single-handedly. I had told my mother to leave me alone. I said no for what seemed like the first time. I began letting my own mother go and cutting our thousand-mile-long umbilical cord.

Little did I know at the time that this was just another in a series of steps to let go of many things, including Laural. I got off the phone and cried and walked, shouting silently and angrily over the way my mother and I had conspired to concentrate all my energy and love into fulfilling her needs. I realized I had even learned my counseling skills from this woman. I could see at a distance her needs, her sad eyes and her dropped shoulders. She was the center of my universe, and I was a satellite that had orbited her with commitment and consistency until that day.

Mom and I didn't talk for over a month. It was wonderful to hear the telephone ring and know I was not going to hear that she or one of my aunts was going into surgery. During this time I kept letting out the tears and the rage and wondering when, if ever, I'd see my parents again. I had severed all contact with my mother. I couldn't explain what was going on, but deep within me miracles were occurring, and little did I know that my parents were unknowingly participating in my maniacal magic.

# 4 GOING DEEPER INTO THE WOUND

*To some extent, the young man,*
*each time he leaves a woman,*
*feels it as a victory, because*
*he has escaped from his mother.*

Robert Bly

I didn't die. At times I thought I was going to. I didn't go mad, although I was sure someone was preparing a room for me at the State Hospital. I didn't let go of Laural or my pain, anger and sadness overnight. But the healing I had been seeking already had begun. By the last part of my thirty-third year it was all the more obvious to me, my friends, my therapists and Laural that I was becoming what I had looked like on the outside for some time.

The things that happened in the final months of that year and the first six months of my thirty-fourth year will sound bizarre at times, and you may not be convinced that I didn't

write this from a small, locked room behind a high fence
with a finely tailored lawn. But I can assure you, I am free to
wander and write without orderlies, doctors and nurses
watching me work.

My body began changing. My physical structure was slowly
reflecting the changes that my inner structures were making.
I began noticing my body more and more. I could feel the
pain and go into it. I could feel the pleasures and cherish
them. I noticed I had a body that was still quite beautiful
though it had been neglected. I began to feel myself as a
whole, as opposed to a pieced-together mechanism without
feeling, that took my head from place to place to be
educated, entertained or bored.

I began noticing other people's bodies at this time as well.
I had been counseling for about eight years and only listening
to my clients' words. While some words are true, most words
are strung togther to keep the stories going and repeat myths.
Unfortunately, most stories (even this one I am telling you
now) omit much of the truth and turn out to be more fiction
than fact. But I would listen. I hope you do. By this thirty-third
year, I stopped listening. I stopped counseling for a while and
started paying attention to my body and others.

I had taken a journey back to my body beginning on
Rachel's table, an experience that served as my physical and
psychological kindergarten. An important part of the journey
came when I realized that I was my mother in many ways and
in other ways I was not. I had sought my mother's face in the
faces of other women, and as soon as I saw it, I flew away in
panic only to begin the search again. Psychological and
spiritual incest is forbidden. By the time I told my mother I
didn't want to see or hear from her for a while I knew I was
truly healing my own mother complex.

Laural knew that I was still trying to use her to replace the
mother who never managed to be a mirror for her son.
Instead my mother was a constant monitor to see if her son
could be all the things she needed him to be.

When I cut the contact with my mother, it hurt her but
immediately helped me. I began seeing Laural more and
more as a separate person, and though we were psychically

connected in ways that still make me shudder, we were no longer playing surrogate "mother and son" games.

After the night that Laural held me for hours as I cried, I began seeing her more often. Days later we went to a movie together. As the film flickered across the screen a sketchy future flashed on and off in my mind. I began thinking it was just possible that we were going to get back together now that I had done so much work on myself and we had been healing our relationship. After the film Laural and I went to a nearby cafe, and once again I saw in her the sadness that was still unreleased.

"Laural, trust me." I reached for her hand but she pulled away. "Talk to me. I'll listen and I'll be there for you."

"John, you've given me no reason to trust you. Every time I do, you hurt and betray me."

The waiter placed two glasses of wine before us. We both looked into our glasses. "I trusted you, didn't I? I told you everything."

"Yes, but you *can* trust me," Laural said as she swallowed her wine and held back the tears.

"Let's go to my house and talk and be together. I'll listen. I love you so much."

We finished our wine in silence, holding hands and not knowing what would happen next. Laural and I went back to my house and shortly after arriving she said, "I just want to be held, John. Can you just hold me?"

"I can do that."

We crawled into bed like we'd done a hundred times before. Lights off and arms snuggly wrapped around each other as if there had never been nor would there ever be a final parting from each other. I held her all night as promised.

The next morning she glowed as I watched the light coming from the window land on her face. Then I began uttering ultimatums. "Laural, I want you to tell Steve we've been together. I also want you to see a therapist with me and I want you to come back."

Laural's countenance sank, and I realized days later that I had completely killed any chance I had of being with this woman. I still had much more work left to do. The next twelve months would be filled with work, remorse and sadness, and a lot of anger that was more than ready to be released.

I began to try to get in touch with the deep anger I felt toward my mother. I decided it was time to see her again and talk to her. I made arrangements to fly to Nashville where my sister lives. Mom was to be visiting there for a few days. I was scared. I was afraid of what I might say and afraid that I wouldn't say all that I needed to. I got very anxious and I was still quite depressed. The day before I left for Nashville I saw my therapist and we discussed my fears.

"Dr. Mason, I'm afraid that she'll just start it all over again, telling me about her diseases or Dad or her sisters, and, worse than that, I'm afraid I'll listen and just fall back into the semicomfortable role of being her counselor. I'm tired of being her counselor. I'm just too tired, period."

"Perhaps she's been doing some thinking herself during the last few months that you've not been in contact," Dr. Mason offered.

I arrived in Nashville, my palms sweaty. I was very much afraid. Mom was waiting at the airport, and we embraced a little coldly but fairly comfortably. The airport was not the place to begin the talk; that would come later. We got in the car to head to my sister's. Before I could say a word, my mother looked deeply into my eyes.

"Son," she said to me. "I've been doing a lot of thinking lately and, well, I guess you have a lot of reasons to be really angry at me, don't you?"

I nearly fell off of my seat. I breathed a deep sigh of relief. "Yes, I do, Mom. I've got a lot that I'm angry about. Why didn't you take me and Kathy and Randy away from Dad's reach? Goddamn it, why didn't you divorce him or at least stop him from abusing us? And you took away my childhood. Why did you make me grow up so fast? I was just a kid. I've been taking care of you since I was five. I've always listened to your complaints about your life. Why didn't you do something if you were so unhappy?"

I went on for an hour. She listened. I raged and cried and cursed. She cried and finally the wall that had been

*Since the mother complex protects one from life, it keeps one from feeling what one feels.*

James Hillman

separating us collapsed. The tears gushed out of both of us and we were still mother and son. The anger that had been released did not remove the primal bond. The trip to Nashville was a success.

Back in Austin the anger and rage kept coming out and the grieving increased. I was changing. Laural commented on how my face was becoming less intense. About this time I decided it was time that I and others began seeing that face that I had been hiding. I had grown my hair long in the early '70s. It usually hung down to my shoulders in long, thick waves and curls. I had managed to avoid the hair trends of the '80s and kept wearing blue jeans and T-shirts to work and out to dinner to say I was different and not conforming. In reality I was mostly hurting and hiding behind my Bohemian image.

I went to the barber and my curls fell onto the floor. As I watched, at first I felt like Sampson. All the power that I fantasized long hair gave me was removed. I felt that I'd lost a part of myself and now was somehow more vulnerable or downright naked. But my head felt lighter, you could see my face, and people said they liked me better with short hair. It took me a long time to get accustomed to the lack of hair, but I finally had to admit it felt good, especially in Austin's humidity. I was changing, and as it says in the ancient Chinese book, the *I Ching, The Book Of Changes*, "Change begins on the outside and works inward."

Next it was time to change my relationship with my father. The father is the hardest figure in the family for many men to deal with. I had given up trying to deal with my own father years before. Before I stopped seeing him, I couldn't walk into a room where he was without the tension becoming so thick you could cut it with a knife. Ten minutes later we would be verbally cutting each other, subtly at first, then violently by the end of my visit.

"When are you going to finish school?" he'd say.

"I don't know," I'd snap back.

"How much will you make when you finally get your Ph.D.?"

"I made $30,000 last year."

"And when are you going to cut that beard off?"

It went on that way for years and got worse. I felt like he had thrown me away long ago and now felt scorn for everything he was and had been. He felt I had thrown him away for my mother. I learned later there was much rivalry between us for her attention.

I had successfully put off really dealing with the anger directed at my father for quite a while. I have noticed that most of the work a man does in self-therapy or psychotherapy is with his mother. Most male therapists have usually dealt with their own mother issues as part of their personal therapy; therefore, they are ready and willing to help another man with his. But few therapists and clients are anything but reluctant to treat the father/son wound. Had it not been for Robert Bly's work in this area, I don't know that I would have ever discovered my true feelings about my father.

I now know the reason why the "father" was such a taboo subject for me. It was because of the tenuous connection I felt to my father in the first place. Unconsciously I did not want to risk severing the small, delicate thread that connected us. If I found out just how angry I was, I might lose him in an even greater way. Hell, I might kill him! So I kept avoiding it until I could no longer deny the importance of the work in this area, as painful and as frightening as it was. I needed to tell my father, not a woman, how I felt. I needed to communicate the hurt I felt toward him for not being at home when I was a boy and for not taking time to get to know me then and for seemingly not wanting to really know me now.

While women — Mom, Dr. Mary Mason, my best friend, Marilyn, and most of all Laural — had helped me so much, I knew that it was now time for me to look to the masculine, the male, perhaps to my father himself, to heal me even more. And yet I wasn't quite ready to face my father. First, I would have to face the fact that I needed more work in the spiritual and physical areas in order to gain the strength I needed to relate differently to my parents and to Laural.

# 5 RETURNING TO THE SPIRIT

> *. . . Spirit is something higher than intellect in*
> *that it includes not only the latter,*
> *but the feelings as well.*
>
> C.G. Jung

I kept trying to get Laural back and at the same time let her go. But the darkness and the depression were still holding on to me as tightly as I was clinging to her. I went deep into my depression when thoughts of suicide kept entering my head like unwelcome intruders. I wrestled with them with the help of Dr. Mason, Laural and others. I finally realized that it was time to increase my efforts to break the cycle of depression and the unwanted, destructive patterns I had created for myself. I had to get more help.

One such helper was a woman named Shamaan, a small-framed black woman who is also part American Indian. She is known around Austin as a very strong medicine woman and healer, having studied the healing arts from Mexican

Curanderos. She uses Jungian dream analysis, Tarot, the *I Ching*, astrology and crystals as well, enabling her to give valuable insight into one's spiritual condition.

I knew that Dr. Mason, with her background in Freudian analysis, was good. But Freudian analysis wasn't completely working for me because it isn't complete in itself. Psychoanalysis involves mostly an intellectual approach to pain. I was also confused. While I was thought of by many as an intellectual, I knew I was more and needed more.

Shamaan Ochaum did a great deal to make me receptive to alternative possibilities and approaches to healing. I knew I could integrate what I was learning from her with my one or two psychotherapy sessions a week. Dr. Mason became comfortable with my synthesizing abilities, although she was at first reluctant. Shamaan began by making me aware of a side of life in which I had once been immersed, but for the last year or two had forgotten and shunned due to my Christian background. She also helped me understand my relationship to Laural in a way that will sound strange to many.

The day before I went to see Shamaan for the first time, I finished reading a play by Sam Shepard. *Fool For Love* had intrigued me after seeing an incredible movie written by him, called *Paris, Texas*. Both touched me in a way that was uncanny and a bit scary, even for one who was fairly comfortable with synchronistic happenings.

The first scene in the movie *Paris, Texas* is an impressively beautiful shot of the Big Bend area of Texan desert. The camera pans the desert, and the first thing seen after the shots of the desert is a man walking determinedly and staring vacantly into the dry void. I began crying as soon as I saw the man walking through the cactus wilderness. My best friend Marilyn, sitting next to me during the show, was quite concerned.

"John," she whispered, "What's wrong? Why are you crying? You don't even know what's happened."

"I know exactly what's happened, Marilyn," I said. "That man could be in the desert walking like that for one reason and one reason only. He hurt the woman he loved and is forced to be separated from her. I know why he's there. I've been there all my life."

As we watched it we found that my plot was the correct one. He had found his soulmate and all but destroyed her. I wept in the darkness throughout the whole movie, wondering if I'd ever leave the desert and find my soul's mate again.

Shepard's play was about a man and a woman who absolutely could not say goodbye to each other and let go. They fought, argued and loved in much the same ways that Laural and I had for years. It was obvious why they caused each other so much misery and yet they stayed together. Finally, when they couldn't stand any more, May (the female character) would leave and Eddie would track her down. I was intrigued to find out the cause of this course of action.

On the day before going to see Shamaan, I had finished reading the play and had found out why those two desperate people stayed together. They not only loved each other in a mostly destructive way, but they also were connected to each other by blood and history — they were brother and sister — same father, different mothers. They were linked to each other's souls.

I was amazed, and the first thought I had as I completed the play was one that I had never before considered. Laural and I were brother and sister! May and Eddie were too. We were linked together in a way that was not logical or rational. We could intuit each other's physical and mental whereabouts without difficulty and had been doing so for a long time. On a subtle level, I had always believed we were what some people called soulmates. Now I was beginning to understand.

The next day I went to see Shamaan. Her house was full of spiritual symbols. Her crystals and paintings all spoke gently as to who she was. I instantly felt warm and comfortable. I was about to find some help and a hidden truth. Shamaan and I sat comfortably close to each other.

"I came here to get some insight and help in a spiritual way," I began. "I've been seeing a psychologist for a year. While she has helped me greatly, I feel we are leaving out an important dimension of my healing. I've been depressed almost all of my life. It's become much worse since the woman I love has left." I went on for only a minute or two more when she suddenly entered into a trancelike state. Moments later she began a spiritual exploration of my deep connection with Laural and our strong intuition about each other.

Shamaan began speaking from her trance, "You and Laural were once twins, brother and sister many lifetimes ago and were separated." She stopped and my heart raced. "You looked for each other, combing the centuries, until you found each other again and married and had as balanced a relationship as a man and woman can have. And then you were separated again. After this separation you, John, went into the desert, and you have been there a long time — alone and unable to believe you will ever find a mate for your soul as loving as your ancient twin sister and wife."

I was stunned and a little frightened at this revelation. Only the day before for the first time, I had felt the brother/sister connection with Laural.

Through my association with Shamaan I came to value a side of religion other than the one I'd been exploring since childhood. I had learned to hide in religion by the time I was six. By nine I was baptized, and it was prophesied by my preacher that someday I'd make a great preacher. By 13 I was out of the church and into the bottle, the same fortress my father had found to shut out the world. By 21 I was back to religion and headed for seminary school, but I somehow got sidetracked by Blake, Coleridge, Emerson, Jung, Lao Tzu and the Buddha. I dove into Eastern Religion and psychology and became a teacher and counselor instead of the preacher my mother wanted.

With Shamaan I explored the *I Ching*, the Tarot, the Runes and astrology, discovering many things. From the *I Ching*, the ancient Chinese book of wisdom, I came to see the need to cultivate a creative receptiveness that I never had before. The *I Ching* guided me to more thoroughly cultivate my feminine side and taught me the necessity of retreating and waiting for right moments to take action, rather than acting in an assertive masculine manner. It taught me the value of Wu

*Tears in floods,*
*sighing and lamenting Good Fortune.*

I Ching

Wei, or actionless action, whereby everything gets done but without striving and struggling. This was very difficult to grasp for a man who felt he always needed to be in control, and that retreat was a sign of giving up. But I kept working with the ideas I was getting through Shamaan and integrating them into the therapy I was getting from Dr. Mason.

There still seemed to be a dimension that was missing. One day Laural and I met at one of our favorite places — Barton Springs. It was summer and I was still as angry as it was hot. Laural and I talked for a while. Then I boiled and the words became scalding water that burned her heart. The anger that was still bottled up inside me seemed ready to come out and destroy everything in sight. I knew that I had to stop hurting Laural. At the end of our time together, I vowed to Laural that I would do something more to release the pent-up anger somewhere other than in her presence. I did. I found Dan Jones.

# 6 RELEASING THE ANGER

*The central demand of the body is to be felt.*

Arthur Jonav

Not only would my therapy experiences finally be rounded out, but my own approach to counseling and therapy would be significantly altered by my encounter with Dan Pearson Jones. Also the work I'd been doing for years with Robert Bly's ideas was going to come alive with this life-filled man. Dan would be the "good father", or perhaps more accurately, the "good uncle". He would serve as my guide and initiator into the adult world via a physical/psycho therapy that he had created using a large dash of Gestalt, a handful of Re-Evaluation counseling, a pinch of yoga, a touch of body work, and other ideas, techniques and training he had received over the last 20 years. He is a master therapist who uses words sparingly.

I chose to see Dan because I had come across an ad in the local holistic magazine. It simply said to come see him when and if it was time to separate or end a relationship and he could help the process. The pain I was causing myself and Laural by not being able to let go thrust me into Dan's counseling room.

I approached his house with a good deal of fear but willingness to try anything or anybody that might help me relieve my pain. I was still experiencing a great deal of depression.

A warm man with a smile that went from ear to ear greeted me as if he'd known me all my life. He gave me a hug that told me I was safe and welcome. Dan stood about 5 feet 10 inches tall and carried himself straight and erect as he walked. I wondered if he could be real, he was so full of energy. I would later find out that he was 48 years old although he looked 10 to 15 years younger, and had more energy than men half his age. Evidently he was doing something right.

We entered his therapy room, and I looked for my spot on the floor that had nothing but carpet and pillows. I found my spot; he found his, and the work on my life began from another perspective. It was work that would last for three months. It was appropriate to where I was and wasn't because it was almost the same place Dan himself had once been many years before as the result of a past and a pain similar to mine.

I began by telling my story. Dan listened but made it evident that he'd heard it before or didn't really need to hear a great deal more. He wasn't impatient with my narrative, but he had learned long ago that just talking can be helpful, but in the long run, it usually doesn't really fix the problem. If it does, it probably won't do so for several years. Dan was definitely not interested in my hanging around for five years and helping him pay off his mortgage. He wanted the same thing I wanted — not to polish my neurosis with words, but nothing less than complete and total change, no matter how much energy and commitment it took to achieve it.

As Dan and I unfolded to each other, I quickly began to see that this man was not like the other three psychotherapists I'd seen. In the first session Dan helped me realize that I was much more angry at nearly everyone and everything than even I had thought, even though the last several months had been filled with recognition of my anger and the occasional ability to show it. The one or two times I had shown my anger I was usually alone, and then only able to show it momentarily. I could not stay with it because I was afraid of it.

"How do you feel about Laural being with another man only a week or two after she left you?" he said with a serious look but a sparkle in his powerful blue eyes.

"It hurts. And I guess I'm a little angry."

Dan quickly grabbed a large pillow next to him and placed it in front of me. "Say, 'I'm angry,' again and let your fist hit the pillow as hard as you'd like."

I got numb and shut down as my fear was greater that moment than my anger. It was my classic symptom of knowing I was angry but not being able to express it. I let my hand fall limply into the pillow. "I'm angry," I squeaked.

"I'm angry!" he said. "Try again this time really letting go into the pillow. You won't hurt it."

"I'm angry." The pillow was still only lightly touched.

"Dan, I can't do this." I grabbed the pillow and threw it to the side. "I can't do this. I can't hit the thing." I started telling my story again about Laural leaving and my alcoholic father and my overprotective mother. Dan didn't force me to hit the pillow. I left his office that first day much more aware that I had a great deal of anger and that I had an even greater inability to let it out. I was really scared of what would happen should I get as angry as I really felt. When Dad was angry I couldn't predict his behavior. Therefore I couldn't control it. Prediction and control were about all that allowed me to survive my crazy childhood. I still felt a need for both to be secure, though both had contributed greatly to my suicidal tendencies and depression.

But the anger was rising to the surface and I was afraid. I decided I would see Dan twice a week, Dr. Mason twice a

*When they are not close to their feelings,*
*they may dismiss it as*
*primitive,*
*unsophisticated,*
*and*
*oversimplified.*

Arthur Jonav

week and Shamaan once every other week. I committed my time, every day and every dollar I could get my hands on. I wanted to try everything and anything that would help heal my wound.

I went back to Dan's office a couple of days later, still depressed and still in need of discharging the anger that I had denied and repressed for such a long time. We started working on my anger by moving back and forth between Laural and my mother. "How do you feel about your mother, John?" he asked.

I started telling him my story about how she possessed me and turned me into a little adult long before I should have been. I told him how she let me take care of her all those years, and how she and I finally had a long talk about it all.

"But how do you feel about that, John?"

"Dan, I don't know," I began crying. I'd been crying for months and then it suddenly dawned on me that one of the reasons I'd cried was because I really didn't know how I felt.

I was angry. I was very angry at Mom and I'd told her so in Nashville. But I had never been able to express it physically. The few times I'd tried, my anger immediately turned into tears or fear.

"John, are you angry at your mom?" Dan gently asked.

"Yes. Damn it, I'm angry!"

"Take this pillow and put your fist into it. Let your anger out. You're not hitting your mother. You're not hurting her; you're letting your anger out into the pillow, which is a way to stop hurting yourself and a way to stop using valuable energy to hold your anger inside you. You could be using that energy for something else." He smiled and handed me a huge pillow.

I looked at the pillow and then at Dan. I remembered the only time I'd ever done anything like this a few months before when I broke the wooden chair into splinters. I was embarrassed and felt awkward. I was reluctant to hit the pillow. I was afraid to let someone, anyone, see me out of control.

"John, just say, 'I'm angry at you, Mom.'" Dan was reassuring with his looks and mannerisms but I was scared to death.

"Dan, if I let this out I don't know what will happen. I've got to keep a lid on it." I was afraid of the unknown, even though I'd seen Laural throw things, scream, not hurt anybody and feel better instantly. I still wasn't sure that I wouldn't destroy Dan's room and even Dan. Dan was sure I wouldn't. He just smiled and waited 'til I was ready.

I began to lightly hit the pillow and under my breath mutter, "I'm angry."

"That's it. Say it so she can hear you."

"I'm angry at you, Mom." My volume increased slightly.

"Again," said Dan.

"I'm angry at you, Mom!" The pillow received a heavy blow. I was still too scared to hit the pillow. Anger was usually not allowed in my family; it was painful and somebody usually hurt when it occurred. I was always taught to hold it in; if you held it in you were somehow stronger than those who couldn't. I had been using my strength to contain my anger for over 20 years; I was worn out and now it was beginning to come out.

"I'm angry, Mom." I slammed the pillow hard but still not as hard as I was angry. Blood was rushing to my face; my pores were opening; I was sweating. My fists were tightly clinched. "I'm angry at you, Mom." My hand came down hard with the words. "I'm angry! I'm angry! I'm angry! . . ."

I was beating the pillow with each word. I was coming alive. Energy was flowing through my whole body. I pounded the pillow for 15 to 20 minutes. I was scared, exhausted, delighted and energized all at the same moment. My breathing was deep and my throat felt open instead of its usual tight feeling.

I finally stopped and looked at Dan. He was still there. I hadn't hurt him. He wasn't afraid. He didn't run away, and his face told me he hadn't rejected me for what I formerly thought to be a ridiculous display of emotion. I began to cry. I was aware that I had consciously, and in front of someone, let myself get out of control enough to get something out I'd wanted to say for a long time. I was finally letting go of the incessant need to hold in my anger.

Dan and I kept working on my anger toward my mother during that session. When it was over I felt tired and strong at the same moment. My body and mind had been connected.

"Dan," I said, "I don't think I can go back to teach my classes after this. I'm exhausted and yet, in a way, I feel great."

"Take a few minutes and breathe." His eyes sparkled. "Your strength will return. If anything, you'll probably have a good deal more energy by this afternoon and you'll sleep better tonight."

"Thanks, Dan, for everything." Tears of joy were running freely down my face. We held each other, and I knew intuitively that I was entering the final stages of my healing.

I left Dan's house and sat by the river for a while thinking about what had happened. I noticed that what I thought was also connected to the sensations I had in my body and particularly my arms. I could feel the healing. My arms told me I had worked out a lot of pain that formerly I could only hold in, or at best talk of.

The work with Dan continued to go well. After several sessions we worked on the anger and sadness I felt about different people I'd loved and hurt and been hurt by. I knew I had to work on a wound left by a beautiful, golden-haired girl from my home town. The girl that I loved had left me and taken a piece of me with her that would take me a long time to get back. I fell madly in love with her when I was 16. We dated on and off for five years. We went to college together in our home town. She became an honor student and I a drunk and dropout. Everybody loved Penny Boone. She was big-boned and attractive and always had a bright smile for everyone.

I tried everything to get Penny to love me, marry me and make love to me. None of the above happened. We got precariously close to all three, and in a way that further destroyed me and my already limited ability to trust people.

I tried to buy Penny's love. I would have resorted to begging, and in a way I did resort to just that. One night when we were 21 we almost made love. Things were going better for us and we were getting closer than we'd ever been.

The evening was quiet and there was a gentle spring breeze
blowing the curtains of my rented house trailer. Penny came
in from a dance class with tights that told me her physical
secrets. I knew I had to make love or die trying. We two
Christians caressed, started to undress, and then she threw
herself off the bed, flew into a rage and told me she never
wanted to see me again as long as she lived. She got dressed
and three months later married a man she hardly knew. At
the wedding she told her mother she didn't know why she
wasn't marrying me.

After that, all women became Penny, and I was angry at that
beautiful woman who never told me why she left that night.
Somehow I believed all woman were capable of doing the
same thing. I didn't begin to see things differently until I had
released what seemed a 1,000 pounds of pent-up pressure
and cried a gallon of tears over the pain of her departure. I
grieved and growled out in anger and sadness in Dan's office
and slowly stopped dreaming of the woman. I finally called
her after not seeing her for years and asked, "Why?" We
talked long distance for five hours. She told me. She was
simply afraid.

Although I had told my Penny story a thousand times, I had
never released my anger until working with Dan..That anger
had helped make all women like Penny, like my mother —
not there for me because they were both afraid.

I tried to make Laural into Penny but couldn't. Laural was
herself. It took a long time to really see this. She was a
woman who sometimes loved too much for her own good
but kept giving me love and staying with me even though she
was no longer able to be my lover. But she never disappeared the way Penny had. I was beginning to feel that
maybe she wasn't going to leave or come back, and this both
delighted and angered me.

Laural and I decided that seeing Dan together might help
both of us. We met early one morning for coffee and shared
our fears. Though she was still seeing and semi-living with
her new lover, we felt we loved each other enough to do
whatever we could to heal each other and our wounded
relationship.

Dan had us tell each other how we were feeling at the moment. We both willingly admitted how afraid we were and how angry we were at the other.

Dan had Laural tell me how she felt. Fifteen minutes later I could honestly say I heard her. She had made herself so clear and laid out her feelings before me like cards on a table. I was amazed at the way she could just say what she felt when she wanted to if I gave her my full attention and didn't interrupt. One thing Laural made clear was that she couldn't be with me until I could express anger appropriately.

It was my turn. I talked for 15 to 20 minutes and barely said anything.

"Are you aware that Laural is not looking at you most of the time you are talking?" Dan asked midway through my monologue and lecture.

"Yes, I noticed. She does that all the time. She doesn't listen to me." I was getting angry and afraid.

"Do you know why she doesn't look at you?" Dan asked.

"Because she doesn't care. She never cared." I began crying.

"Laural, tell John why you're not looking at him when he's talking to you," Dan said.

"He's not talking to me. He's talking at me. He's preaching, accusing and trying to make me feel like a bad person."

"Goddamn it, Laural, that's not true," I said. "I'm just trying to tell you how I feel, and you're not paying attention." As I spoke the words Laural looked away.

"John, Laural's right," Dan said to me. "The anger you feel toward her is keeping you from communicating your feelings. I think Laural is willing to listen and she's very interested in what you have to say if you can say it in a way that doesn't threaten or accuse her. Isn't that correct, Laural?"

"John, I love you or I wouldn't be here. I want to hear you, but the things you're saying aren't true. I've always wanted to listen."

I saw that she and Dan were right. For the first time I realized why she never looked at me when I talked. I thought it was something lacking in her. It was something lacking in me. I had never been able to really talk to Laural and I still wasn't able to. Somehow I did manage to say something to her during that session that she could hear.

"Laural, I love you," the tears rolled down my cheeks, "and I've never been able to tell you how I feel because I'm afraid I don't know how."

Dan watched Laural and me looking at each other and holding hands as I wept.

"I never really knew until today that John loves me. But I now know that he does," she said.

"I don't think I need to see you again, Laural, for a while. If you'd like to talk some more, feel free to call. And, John, I guess I'll see you next week." Laural stepped into another room as Dan and I made another appointment.

Upon leaving, Dan hugged us both. I realized that I had much more work to do. I also realized how much Laural loved me and I her, even though I couldn't express myself to her. I had to figure out, for the life of me, why I couldn't talk to her. I had to figure that out and overcome it.

# 7 FINDING MY FATHER

*You beat time on my head*
*with a palm caked hard by dirt,*
*Then waltzed me off to bed*
*still clinging to your shirt.*

My Papa's Waltz, Theodore Roethke

At first I could not understand why I was less able to talk to the woman that I loved than anyone else. When I'd try to tell Laural how I felt, the words would get so jumbled and contorted. I'd talk for two hours only to end up draining both of us and still not saying what I really intended. I was still out of touch with my body and therefore my feelings. I wasn't able to say what I wanted to say.

It was shortly after my session with Laural that I discovered I had never been comfortable talking to those I loved. I wasn't as a child. For the most part, Mom talked to me and I listened. I never learned to tell my father how I felt for fear of rejection and ridicule, or because he was never at home long enough to hear what I needed to say even if I found the courage to tell him.

I realized that I had overdeveloped my ability to talk to anyone other than the people who counted the most. If enough of them listened, it would make up for not being heard as a child. I could lecture with eloquence to unknowns, tell my troubles to strangers, but when it came time to talk to Laural, I might as well have been mute.

I kept examining this inability to communicate with Laural. Finally, after visiting Dan's office for the eighth or tenth time, I realized that I needed to talk to my father as much as or more than to Laural. I needed to tell him what I really felt. I had let go of a lot of anger toward my mother and told her how I felt. The communication problem with my mother had begun to seriously and steadily improve.

In preparing to talk to my dad, I realized how much he and Laural were alike. This was startling! I had always been aware that Laural reminded me of my mother. But no one had ever told me or perhaps seen a connection between a man's lover and his father. I could list a dozen character traits, manner-isms and behavior patterns of theirs·that were very similar. They were both distant people who didn't talk much at all about feeling. Neither of them were very good with words. Mom and I were great wordsmiths. They were both introverts — Mom and I were always going out to everyone; Dad and Laural worked with their hands — Mom and I worked in our heads. This list kept growing. By being with Laural not only was I getting a second chance to be with my mother, but I also was maintaining a continuity of feeling and connection to my father.

I knew I had to talk to my dad if I were ever going to really talk to Laural or, for that matter, any woman I ever loved. I saw that if your parents don't seem interested and don't take time to listen, you tend to think no one will. I began by talking to Dad in Dan's therapy room and in my living room. Dan would help me get started by digging into painful memories and going back to the time when I needed Dad the most and he wasn't there. A lot of anger and rage came up and out. My depression was lessening its grip. As I talked to my imaginary father, tears and anger were released, and so was the tightness and constriction I had felt in my throat for years. The more I really told him how I felt, the easier it became to do so. Communication between Laural and me immediately improved. After not having seen him for four years, I decided that it was time to go to my father and talk to him face to face, fear to fear.

The last time I had seen him was at a Christmas get-together. He was drunk and obnoxious. I left vowing never to be in that man's presence again until he stopped drinking. I had put up with it as a child, but I decided I didn't have to subject myself to his abuse any longer.

However, I knew that I needed to make one more genuine effort to contact my father, and by doing so, contact something in me that I had given up long ago. I needed my dad if I were to break through the communication walls I had built between myself and the ones I loved. I also knew that I was ready to recover the father within me who was an inseparable part of my deepest self. For years I had tried to rebel against this part of myself by becoming in touch with my feminine self, growing my hair long and taking jobs that were the direct opposite of his. My dad was in me. I knew it, and Laural knew it. I thought that I hated him and that part of me, but I was beginning to see that I deeply loved that part of me that was my dad.

One night, in a deep state of depression (though not nearly as deep as several months before) I decided that I had to go home. I had to see my father. For the first time in my life I knew I needed my dad. I made a call home and Dad answered:

"Dad," I started crying, "I need to come home."

"Come on, Son." I heard Dad swallow the lump in his throat.

It was fall and I was flying home to see my father. I was frightened by the possibilities, and yet I knew that I had to pursue this course of action if I were ever to truly heal.

As I flew to Florida, I kept remembering scenes from childhood: my father drinking and driving, getting stopped by the police and handing me his bottle to hide . . . at age six my dad and mom placing me on a bus to make a 24-hour journey by myself . . . his beating my sister . . . at nine seeing him go for my mother's throat in a fit of anger. Memories came back as I neared Florida.

There was a deep sadness rising in me for a father I felt I had lost a long time ago. The sadness was also because I was so aware of how much I had missed this man who had marked my psyche and soul and motivated me to turn my back on masculinity and maleness. But for the first time, I was keenly aware that I desperately loved this man and needed him in my life, if possible, before he or I died.

I looked into the dark southern skies as we flew and cried silently. At times I went to the plane's restroom to fully release the grief I was feeling. I cried on and off all the way to Tampa.

As we landed I was so nervous I could hardly contain myself. My palms were sweating. What would I say to him after all these years? What would he say to me? Would he be able to deal with me? I was falling apart. The reason I was there was to get put back together. What if we couldn't be together? I was afraid we'd just argue again. I kept repeating these questions until they became mantras as we made our descent.

Finally the airplane came to a halt. Mom had called and said Dad would be there waiting for me. I wondered if he really would or if he'd decide to send Mom. Years before, when I'd call home and he'd answer, he'd quickly give the phone to my mother. I needed to see my father so much more than my mother.

I slowly walked off the plane and into the arrival gate. I gulped back the tears because I didn't want Dad to see me crying. As I walked, the pressure in my chest increased and my legs went limp. As I passed the faces looking for someone other than me, I scanned the crowd. My eyes landed on a tall man with a slightly protruding stomach who was handsome for his age. I hardly recognized him, and yet in many ways it was like looking at a future picture of myself.

He saw me. He smiled and a tear ran down his face. I walked up to him, dropping my bag, my image and my anger and fell into his arms. We held each other tightly trying to forget the years and the distance. We wept as people passed by not knowing that a son had found his lost father.

Dad and I talked all the way home. I listened and so did he. There was a great deal that needed saying after so many years of silence, yelling and misunderstandings. By the time we arrived at my parent's home, I was exhausted. I hadn't been sleeping much and so I went to bed.

The next morning we were up early. Dad and I sat in the front yard, talking at one another just like old times. We were each trying to defend ourselves against the other's words that were like arrows being shot from ancient bows. He was pushing all the right buttons and I was pushing back. The old pattern was in place.

"I don't want to spend my life just making money." My breathing became shallow.

"What's wrong with money? It put you through school, didn't it? Bought your clothes and food — didn't it?" His face turned red as he spoke.

"Dad, I didn't say it was wrong. It's just that you devoted your life to getting it and I don't want to."

"There's nothing finer than to be able to go to any restaurant and order anything you want and know you can pay for it, or walk into a bank and get a loan to buy a new car or . . ."

It went on like this for an hour or so before I realized what we were doing — more of the same. I got up and went inside to talk to Mother while she fixed breakfast.

I tried to avoid Dad most of the day, just as I did as a kid. I wanted to be near him and yet I wanted to stay out of his way and his wrath. When I was around Dad, I was a boy and he was the man — I was the son and he was the father. Even though we both stood six feet and one inch tall, he looked bigger than me.

That evening I was depressed and going deeper into darkness. The trip simply was not giving me what I'd come for. Dad was just like he always had been, and so was I in spite of my desperate desire to change.

We went out to dinner. Dad was going to impress me with his monetary muscle again and treat me to the "finest seafood in Tampa." He tried to order for me, and then when that failed, he tried to force-feed me food that, in his opinion, I should have ordered.

"Here, Son, try this. You'll love it," he smiled.

"Dad," I was getting tense, "I don't like raw oysters."

"But they're great." Putting the oysters on my plate, "Try just one."

He kept this going until finally, in a burst of anger, I yelled, "Dad, I'm going to take you and dip you in this bowl of butter if you don't cut it out and calm down."

The anger came out. I got up, excused myself and walked to the parking lot in the rain thinking about what I'd said and getting more and more depressed. The trip just wasn't working. I had to talk to Dad, really talk or go back home earlier than I'd planned. I went back into the restaurant.

"Can we please go?" I said with a cracked voice. I got behind the wheel of the car and we started home. The tension was high and I felt something had to happen. "I'm going back to Austin in the morning."

"Son, you just got here," Mom said, looking back at Dad who sat silently in the back seat.

"Come on, Son," Dad said, "I just wanted to show you a good time. I know you've been going through a lot lately. Your mother told me about Laural. We can eat good food, and tomorrow we'll go to the Busch Garden. Just try to have a good time while you're here."

"Goddamn it, you're going to listen to me," I said hoarsely, my eyes fixed on the rain-slick street. "I didn't come here to have a good time or argue with you or eat your goddamn oysters. I came here to see you, to talk to you. I'm falling apart. I've been falling apart for years. I need you to talk to me and listen to me." Now I was screaming at the top of my voice and tears were getting in my mouth as I choked and drove on.

"Pull over, Son, let me drive," my mother was softly saying.

"Yeah, Son, take it easy. Pull over and let your mother drive. We'll talk."

*You have to lose your mind
to come to your senses.*

F. Perls

"No, goddamn it, not until you listen to me," I retorted. "If we don't talk, I mean really talk to one another, I don't know what I'm going to do. But I do know I'm going home and you're never going to see me again as long as you live. I've got to get you to understand me, Dad." I pleaded. "I've got to understand you."

"Okay," he conceded. "Just pull over and let your mother drive and we'll talk."

I pulled into a gas station and swapped places with Mom. We began a talk that lasted five hours. Mom said little. Dad and I talked, cried, held each other, screamed at each other, and nearly punched each other out more than once. The anger was coming up and out of both of us, and so was the sadness. I knew there was much more anger in me than Dad could deal with. But we started.

We were all drained and depleted. Mother had parked the car hours before in the driveway, but we stayed in it to talk. Finally we could go no further.

"Don't you wish we could just return to the days of childhood when everything was so simple and we didn't have a care in the world?" Dad said, trying to close the conversation on a light note. He looked at me and a final tear for that night fell from both our eyes. "But then," he said, looking at me sadly, "I guess you wouldn't know about those times, would you, Son? I'm sorry."

The next day I cut my beard of 12 years to look at my face and to show that face to the parents I was beginning to know.

# 8 THE DREAMS, THE ANIMALS: POWER RETURNS

*There is only one thing which is indispensable
for anything we do . . . The Spirit.*

Journey to Ixtlan, Don Juan

By the time I left Florida I knew I'd come a long way from
where I'd been, and my dad and I were closer to healing our
relationship and our own separate wounds. I also knew that
there was still a great deal more to be done. I knew that I had
told Dad a lot, but that I still carried a great deal of
unexpressed anger and grief over having lost my one shot at
childhood.

On my return to Austin I sensed another shift in my ability
to communicate with Laural and others. It was noticeable to
Laural as well. I was stronger, more sure of myself and
clearer. The power that I had regained through the
experience with my dad was making me feel much more
able to let go of Laural and get on with my life.

I was beginning to see a return of my own forfeited power through the dreams I was having and my interactions with the animal world. I knew it to be absolutely necessary for my healing.

During this year and a half of change, growth and discovery I found that I was experiencing the physical world in a way I had not done since childhood. As I made the journey from my head back to my body, I began to see, hear, touch, taste and smell things in a heightened way. It has been suggested in Edgar Allen Poe's writings and in folktales that just before one goes mad, he experiences the world of the senses in this way. Fritz Perls once said, "You have to lose your mind to come to your senses."

The pain that I was experiencing was equal in intensity to the sensations I was getting from the natural world and my dream life.

As I mentioned in the second chapter, two major dreams presented me with the images of the mouse, the hawk and then later the wolf, in the dream where I howled like a wolf when I was told my father had died. The wolf was to become a special power animal in my dreams and would help heal my wounds.

Right after making my trip to see my father, I had a dream in which I was kneeling by a rushing stream, drinking water. When I looked up, directly across from me stood a beautiful black and grey wolf. We looked at each other for a few moments. Then I asked him to cross the stream and give me his power. He crossed and I embraced him. We played and scuffled, enjoying each other's company. As we wrestled, I knew I had acquired the power of the wolf to see me through the coming months of my healing and letting go. The image of the wolf would appear many times as the weeks turned into months. I began noticing books and articles on wolves and encountering the wolf's domesticated cousin, the husky, everywhere, especially when I was feeling low or powerless.

One day a woman walking her husky passed me. She looked at her dog's blue eyes and then mine and simply said, "If you were an animal, this is what you'd be," pointing to her dog as she walked on. During the course of the next few

*The butterfly counts not months but moments,
and has time enough.*

Rabindranath Tagore

months I howled many nights for my mate and for my sadness.

The butterfly also became important to my healing. Friends, especially Laural, often noticed them in our immediate vicinity when we were talking. They would often light on me. I found this amazing at first, but stayed open to any healing possibilities they might represent, remembering that five or six years before I had one of my first out of body experiences with a butterfly.

One day, while I was sitting alone on my parent's boat dock reading, a butterfly appeared and landed on my big toe. I decided to follow an intuition I had the moment it landed: I would attempt to exchange bodies with this beautiful creature. It inched its way up my body until finally it came to rest on my hand. It stayed there and I stroked it gently, and we made the exchange. All this took about 45 minutes. It is rare for a butterfly or a man to sit in one position for that long. I experienced the interior world of a butterfly and then gently slipped back into my body, having learned unspeakable lessons.

Butterflies were now appearing at just the right moment to remind me of the things I learned that day and forgotten.

While out of town, Laural had left her car for me to drive. I looked in and found a butterfly floating calmly, looking for an escape route. The next day there were two butterflies floating from front to back and window to window. I had no idea how they had entered because all the windows were up. I let them out and watched them take their freedom. The most incredible encounter came more recently as I was working on the early drafts of this manuscript. It was during the winter, with gas heaters blazing. I watched as a butterfly fluttered through my living room and landed on my desk, as if to bless my work and remind me of my changes from caterpillar to butterfly — a Flying Boy into a man.

The next animal that played a significant teaching role was the blackbird, or at least the Texas version of it called the grackle. One evening in the early stages of my healing, I was walking to one of the half dozen U.T. campus theaters. Outside the theater the trees were filled to overflowing with screaming grackles. This happens two or three times a year in Texas, usually in the fall and early summer. As I watched and listened, I intuitively knew that even though this was not a supernatural act, they were communicating a warning: "Don't go into the theater." I ignored this, thinking that I was being overly romantic or ridiculous.

But, the grackles' cries were ominous as I entered the theater and I knew I shouldn't be there. And suddenly I knew it was because I would see Laural and Steve! I could choose to leave before they got there and spare myself some pain or stay and hurt. I stayed and I hurt as she and Steve walked into the only movie we three would see some portion of together. I was only able to stay for 15 or 20 minutes and when I left, I found the birds had done the same. Not one remained in the trees. Some intellectuals might call me a solipsist (the doctrine that the self is the only object of real knowledge), but I have been called worse things.

Later that year the grackles increased their messages to me in the form of a very wounded member of the family. The area outside of the small bakery where I went early every morning to have coffee and to write in my journal was a bird hunting ground for food crumbs. I noticed one grackle in particular who had a bad leg. It was all gnarled and twisted as he hobbled from one speck of food to the next, never getting there quite fast enough before one of his fellow feathered friends descended on his breakfast.

I watched this bird nearly every day for over a year. Finally I began feeding it. His wounded leg reminded me of my own figurative inability to walk well on both legs. But when the bird was in the air, he didn't look wounded at all. He flew as well as the next, and as well as I did.

The bird was a physical reminder to me of the myth of Hephaestus, an ancient Greek myth Robert Bly relates in his men's workshop. Basically it is a story of how the son is wounded and crippled by the father. Hephaestus is the son of Hera and Zeus. Briefly what happens is that Hera conceives the boy to get revenge on Zeus for his having angered her. Hephaestus and Zeus never got along well, and one day Zeus, in a fit of rage, throws his son out of the heavens (the house) and the boy falls a long way and is crippled from then on.

Every time I saw the blackbird I recalled this story. I kept feeding it, and in the process kept healing myself, in part by reducing the distance from my father and my own masculinity by reducing the distance between myself and this bird.

A few months ago the blackbird hobbled up to where I sat. It took food from my hand and flew away three consecutive times. Somehow I knew I really had come to terms with my crippled self in those moments. By doing so I no longer felt crippled, but still close enough to being disabled to feel the bird's wound by remembering my own. I was healing.

A few months later, while doing some research on the religion of American Indians, I discovered an interesting and relevant fact in Joseph Epes Brown's book, *The Spiritual Legacy of the American Indian*. This fact seemed to support my encounters with animals and their appearances in my dreams:

> Animals were created before human beings (Indian creation myth), so they have a certain proximity to the great Spirit. In them the Indian sees actual reflections of the qualities of the Great Spirit, which serve the same function as revealed scriptures in other religions. They are intermediaries or links between humans and God.

Only weeks later I met with a friend who knew I was interested in Native American astrology. He gave me a book called *The Medicine Wheel* by Sun Bear. I read most of it and then turned to the section that told what my totem animals (animals unique to one's time of birth that hold special and spiritual significance) were. To my surprise (I am always surprised, no matter how often this kind of thing happens) my totem animals were the butterfly and the raven.

In the meantime, the tears kept coming. The anger was being released. The animals gave their nonverbal messages. And the dreams kept me on "the royal road to the unconscious".

Two years ago as I entered this process, one of the first dreams I had, told me a great deal in not more than one or two rapid eye movements. Here is my journal entry:

Last night I dreamed my father and I were fighting each other with our own separate pairs of crutches.

It was shortly after this dream that Laural left. The woman I had used as a crutch was gone, and the father who had crippled me appeared crippled himself.

After a few months I had one of the most healing dreams I ever had up to that point in time. I recorded it as follows:

I entered a small room with several people standing around. There was a beautiful baby on the floor (preverbal age). He was talking but no one was listening or else no one could hear him except me. He told me to come closer. I put my ear close to his mouth. He said simply, "You can love now."

Several months later I had and noted another dream in my journal:

I took a trip into the forests of a South American country with an old man and his son. The man was a wood craftsman. We went by canoe to a city where a wealthy woman owned an elegant shop. She wanted the old man to buy something from her. I looked at the various objects in her antique store while they talked. Finally he decided not to buy anything she was selling. We all left together, the little boy, the man and me.

About this same time I was studying the *I Ching*. I had a dream in which one of the Chinese characters in the *I Ching* called "The Marrying Maiden" appeared in my dream. The maiden said, "In the *I Ching* I often come as a concubine or a female slave, servant or wife." In the dream Laural was the concubine coming to me for marriage. As she stood before me I looked over my left shoulder and saw the woman I loved. She too was Laural. I sent the concubine away and spoke to the one I loved.

After a year of work, tears and healing I began trying to write a book about what had been happening. At first, due to my insecurities about who I was and what I had been through, I tried to write it as a dissertation on Robert Bly's work. I wanted to make it academic so that I could hide behind intellectual jargon. But I could not get started. And though the book would not really get started until nearly a year after this next dream, it was this dream that helped me see it was time to leave academia and to finally tell the truth.

I dreamed that I met a spiritual and intellectual guide. She was beautiful and had a beard. She was part Hindu and part American Indian. She simply said, "You can write your book now that I am here, and you have to do well because it is God's book."

The dreams did not cease. During the last several months I've had many nocturnal and early morning messages from the unconscious that have continued my growth and healing. Those mentioned were some of the more important ones that came while I was dealing with my father, my mother, my anger as well as my sadness and my feelings about Laural and women and men in general.

As the dreams began decreasing in intensity and number, sleep was increasing. For years I had wrestled with insomnia, waking two to six times a night after taking one to three hours to fall asleep.

My deep depression had disappeared. The tension was leaving my body and this was obvious in a number of ways, particularly when I went swimming. It was less of a struggle to stay afloat since I was more buoyant. I knew this was in part due to my being much less angry at a father who taught me how to swim by throwing me off a pier.

The darkness was leaving my face and my demeanor was more often light and less intense and frightening to others. My voice lowered an octave as the released tears and anger relaxed my vocal cords and my testosterone level increased (studies have shown that when men cry, they increase their testosterone level).

By releasing anger, which reduces the tension and grieving over the past pain, traumas and losses, I could tell my physical and psychic structures were shifting. My shoulders, which had been slowly shifting further and further towards the floor without effort on my part, were coming back to rest in a more structurally correct position. I was no longer carrying my mother and my father on my back. Body, mind and spirit were healing simultaneously from the work I had been doing for the last two years.

During this time Laural and I saw each other occasionally. I would still fall into old behavior patterns, but the need to control and manipulate was waning. More often we were able to communicate our feelings to each other with a mixture of sadness, anger and genuine love. All the while I was letting go more and more of the need to cling to her due to my neediness and my inability to separate from her and, to a lesser degree, from my mother and father. I kept working, reading, receiving body work and psychotherapy. I changed my diet, increased the amount of time spent exercising and kept trying to say goodbye to the woman I loved, allowing myself to do so in my own time.

Most of the time I felt good. I was beginning to experience what it meant to be happy and really healthy. I was feeling my feelings and my body as never before. I was beginning to take pride in my looks, my abilities, my accomplishments and my masculinity. I was beginning to love myself, and I slowly began seeing to it that I got what I needed, by being able to give it to myself or ask others for it.

I decided it was time to go back to an occupation that I had loved though had never really committed to: counseling. However, I decided to wait until I was sure that I was healed enough to provide the kind of care, concern and counseling I needed to give, without tearing myself down in the process. A few more things had to happen. They did and they served as signs that it was time.

# 9

# A HEALING SYNCHRONISTIC MEETING

*Robert Bly is a cantankerous, hulking, white-haired,*
*57-year-old poet who looks like a cross between a*
*grizzly bear and a wizard.*

L.M. "Kit" Carson

As I mentioned earlier, I had been following Robert Bly's work for four years. Finally it was being realized in my own life. I was cutting my own umbilical cord to my mother and was getting back the psychosexual energy that she stole from me. I was getting in touch with my own "deep masculinity" and was quickly becoming proud to be male. I was spending an equal amount of time with men where previously I had trusted only women enough to share my secrets and pain. I was learning to trust men and open up to them, thanks to Robert Bly's essays, interviews and poems. I had nothing but respect and possibly a little hero worship for the man who had so influenced and helped heal my life.

Through experience and my reading, I had become an expert on Bly, the poet from Minnesota. I knew his work backwards and forwards. Yet I had never met the man until September, 1985, a year and one-half after having begun my transformation through grieving and releasing anger.

One cool evening in September I would be initiated into the world of the healthy by one powerful person.

A very good friend and mentor, Dr. Betty Sue Flowers, helped set the stage for our meeting. She had been encouraging me in my work and transformation for nearly a year by reading what I was writing in preparation for this book. She was also very familiar with Robert Bly's work. Betty Sue helped arrange a scholarship for me to attend the conference. I received notice that I could come and hear Bly free of charge as a guest. I was delighted, to say the least.

The conference and dinner were to be held in a small city only an hour's drive from Austin. As the days quickly passed, I knew I was becoming increasingly anxious about meeting my mentor. The day came. I was nervous but decided I would not make this mortal man into a sacred cow, no matter how much his life and work had meant to me.

When I arrived at the meeting site, I was only minimally nervous, but the tension soon increased.

"Hello," I said anxiously to the hostess. "I'm John Lee. I received a scholarship from the society to attend this conference with Bly." We looked for my name tag among dozens of names of psychiatrists and psychologists. Mine wasn't among them.

"No problem. We'll make you one. We were expecting you," she said and smiled. My pulse rate decreased for a moment. I looked at the room full of seats and only a few dining tables. I immediately assumed I would be put in the back and not be served dinner after the conference.

"Where should I sit?" I asked, thinking I already knew.

"Oh, you'll be sitting up front," she smiled again.

"Up front. You mean the front where the folded chairs are lined up?"

"No. I mean up front by the speaker." She was getting a little irritated at my slowness to grasp what she was saying to me.

"Excuse me. Where exactly should I sit?"

"You see the table up front by the speaker? That's where your seat is."

"By the speakers?"

"Yes." She was looking at me wondering how someone so retarded could be given a scholarship. "The table right by the speaker stand is where you'll be sitting. You'll be eating dinner at Bly's table."

I nearly swallowed my tongue trying to thank her for her benevolence. I walked up, and sure enough, my name card was at the seat to Bly's immediate right and across from the man who was responsible for getting Bly to speak. I couldn't believe it. I would be two feet away from the man as he spoke and at his elbow as he ate. I was stunned. I had not expected anything like this. I couldn't imagine what I was going to say to him. I went back to the hostess.

"Are you sure I'm supposed to be right by Bly?" I stammered, almost hoping for a reprieve.

"Yes. I'm sure."

"Thanks."

I went and took my seat and waited anxiously for the talk to begin.

Finally Bly entered. He was taller and younger looking than I expected. He sat down at the table and didn't even look at me. He talked to his friend who was getting ready to introduce him. Bly sat there and didn't even see me. I thought to myself, "What if the man I've admired all these years is an arrogant ass-hole?"

Bly got up and began his two-hour discussion of what it means to be a male in the '80s after having lost touch with our masculinity at the time of the Industrial Revolution and losing our fathers to offices and factories. As he talked, I watched him in awe, listened and already knew everything he was saying.

Thirty minutes into his talk Bly was making more and more eye contact with me as I sat watching an unofficial authority on masculine psychology. By the end of his talk and poetry reading I knew why I was there. Fate had not been solely responsible for my position at his table. I was there

*. . . like a ship
that took me safely
through the wildest storm of all.*

Rilke

because I deserved to be. It became clear to me as he talked that I was probably the only person in the room that knew his ideas almost as well as he himself; I was a living example of many of those ideas that came out of his own life experiences and from his studies of the work of C.G. Jung, world mythology, fairy tales and a myriad of other sources.

Finally the talk was over. I still did not know what I would say, but I was no longer afraid. I had earned my place beside him. After dozens of people approached him to thank him or have a book signed, he seated himself beside me, looked me straight in the eye, and said, "I certainly enjoyed your pleasant face while I was talking. It made me feel good, like I was talking to an old friend. You've heard everything I said today before, haven't you?"

"Yes, I have."

"Why did you come here tonight then?"

"Just to say thank you and ask for a hug. I've been following your work for four years and I thank you for who and what you are and for what you're doing for men and women all over the country."

We stood and embraced each other, and I knew that I was holding a spiritual father or perhaps an uncle who had initiated me into the world of adult men.

We sat down and in between admirers coming up to question or dote on him, we talked and talked. I told him I was working on a book that he would figure in prominently. As the end of the evening neared I knew it was time to leave the man I so admired, and as we hugged each other once again, Bly gave his blessings to the work I had done on my life and the work I'd call *The Flying Boy: Healing the Wounded Man.*

"I'm sure we'll meet again," we both said as we said goodbye.

# 10 ACCEPTING MY FATHER, FINDING MYSELF

*. . . the child would remain without a mirror,
and for the rest of his life would be seeking
the mirror in vain.*

Alice Miller

I left the conference feeling strong and sad. I knew that I had just completed another stage in my growth, and I could never again return to many of my old ways. I was also sad because I could not share this event with the person I most wanted to tell. It was my first rite of passage among many to follow.

I knew it was time to open a new counseling practice that would bring together the ideas I got from Bly and Jung, some training in Gestalt therapy and the techniques found in Harvey Jackins' Re-Evaluation counseling. I made a commitment to work only with men for a while, to become the best possible helper to men and women who needed to let out both anger and grief, and to help men reclaim their denied

masculinity and their anima. I only had a couple more things
to do before I'd be ready. I had to see my father one more
time and connect with him on a deeper level.

During a few months before meeting Bly, Dad and I
worked at getting closer, a result of the visit I had made to
Tampa. I was still feeling bad about losing Laural, and Dad
knew it. He began calling me just to talk, something he'd
never done before — ever. One particular night I was sadder
than usual, though not depressed. The unmanageable
depression I had suffered for more than two decades was
over. I was just sad. Sadness, I was learning, was manageable
and did not cripple. I was at home alone when Dad called.

"Hello, Son. I just called to see how you were doing." His
voice was distant but strong.

"Dad, I'm not doing really well right now," I answered.
"I'm really sad tonight."

"Still missing Laural? John, Son, I hope you get over this.
You'll love again."

"Dad, what should I do?" I blurted out. "I've never asked
your advice on anything before, but I need to know what I
should do. I love this woman so much. What should I do?"

"Son, I'm going to tell you," he began, speaking slowly,
with obvious deliberation. "You should love Laural the way
your mother loves me. Not the way I love, but the way your
mother loves and the way Laural loves. John, remember your
mother left me and filed for a divorce a few years ago? Son,
I knew that she did that because she loved me. She loved me
enough to let me go. I can't love that way. Maybe you're too
much like me, but if I can tell you anything, I'd say love
Laural like your mother loves me. Let her go, Son."

I started crying. The words were not only true, they were
wise and they were coming from my father. "Thanks, Dad."
My voice steadied, "I'll try. Thanks for being there for me. I
love you, Dad."

"Oh, Son, I love you, too."

I came one step closer to my father that night and took
another step away from Laural. I decided now was the time to
really start writing and counseling. This was October of 1985

and I had just turned 34. I started trying to write. And all kinds of fears started emerging, particularly about Laural and Dad.

In November I began to focus on my writing. Bill Stott, an American Studies professor, writer and teacher of writing, (see his last book, *Write To The Point*, Doubleday) had been supervising my writing for years. I learned a great deal from this man. He agreed to read my work. In the process we became close friends.

The first attempts were momentary setbacks. I kept hiding behind academic writing and Robert Bly. I wanted to write a scholarly book on Robert Bly's life and work. I see now that this was the last remnant of a false self still trying to satisfy a need for security. Dr. Stott and Dr. Flowers kept reading my work and asking me when I was going to put my story on paper. For several months I played as if I didn't know what they were talking about. I was afraid to tell my story. I knew it meant telling people who I really am. So I kept hiding behind a third-person academic voice and couldn't write a word worth reading. I kept struggling and turning in garbage. Dr. Stott was kind, as was Dr. Flowers. The first chapter was written six times. Each time it got better because something in me was listening to them, and more and more of me came out between the lines of the pseudoscholar's words.

Finally, one day in therapy with Dan Jones, he began working on my body by doing some acupressure. As I lay on the floor, it suddenly came to me that the reason I could not write the book was twofold. I could let go of my defenses, the need to please and the need to sound like someone I wasn't. But there was still the problem of my inability to let Laural go. I knew that day I wouldn't be able to write this story until I had let Laural go.

The second reason, related to the first, was that I was not only afraid to tell the world who I was and how I had been hurt by the people I love, but I was afraid that the words would hurt my father with whom I had just recently reconnected. I would also have to love him enough to let go, and yet I was afraid that what I had to say about him would cause us to separate again. I knew that while I had to write the book, I did not want to lose my dad in the process. I was afraid to let go.

I wept. I then and there decided that I could not write until I had worked through these two remaining issues.

It was December. I called Dad and told him I was coming home for my first family Christmas in five years. I would celebrate the birth of a niece with my family, further my connection with my father and, at the same time, separate from him.

There were no tears on the plane and very little fear as I flew to Tampa. As I deplaned, my father and brother stood like bookends waiting for me. As we drove home I could feel a slight tension among the three of us as Randy drove faster than I cared for, and Dad did more back-seat driving than Randy cared for. When we arrived the whole family was there. My sister with the new baby, and her husband were standing by my grandmother and mother. All were a welcome sight.

Christmas Day was easy. We exchanged presents. One of the presents I received was a sign and symbol of my growth and healing as well as my father's. When it came time for me to open my present from Dad, he appeared nervous and excited and was already a bit teary-eyed. (Even as a boy, Christmas was the only time I would see my father cry, and then he'd try to hide it or joke it away.) I couldn't imagine what was in the box that was making him so excited. As I ripped off the paper and opened the box, I burst into tears and so did Dad. Surrounded by white cotton was my grandfather's silver pocket watch. Dad had always known that I had loved his father more than any man, including himself in some ways. He gave me something that day beyond a timepiece. He gave me something of himself and an understanding that could not be put into words. We held each other and cried.

After the colored paper was picked up and the hugs exchanged, my dad needed a drink. He had been purposely trying to limit his drinking that day, in large part for me. The last Christmas five years before had been drowned in alcohol. This Christmas he was sober.

"I need a drink. Ya'll excuse me just a second," he said, walking toward the kitchen.

Dad's honesty about his need struck something in me. He was not trying to hide his alcoholism nor his pain. As he went for the cupboards, I spontaneously said something totally unplanned.

"Dad, pour me one, too."

My mom nearly dropped the dish she was washing. She looked at me with surprise and then understanding. She looked at Dad, who was even more shocked as he slowly poured us each a shot of bourbon. I walked up to my father. We looked into each other's blue eyes. Dad and I raised our glasses together. "Here's to you, Son." He said looking me in the eyes.

"To you, Dad."

At that moment I fully knew the pain, anger, sadness and frustration my father must have felt all those years, and I wanted him to know I understood and in many ways had felt much the same. As we lowered our glasses he looked at me silently for a moment. I knew I loved him unconditionally.

"Care for another?" he asked.

"No thanks — one's plenty," I said setting the glass on the counter.

He quickly poured himself another one, knocked it back and put up the bottle for the rest of the evening. Our understanding was out in the open and would never be hidden again.

A few days after Christmas I reached an even deeper understanding of my father and myself. Mom and I had been talking during the days my father worked. One afternoon he came in and found the power off in the house. Mother and I checked everything we could to find the cause. Dad was tired from a job he's hated for years. What transpired over the next two hours made me confront to its fullest what I had wanted to ignore. And that truth was just how much I was like my father, and to a much lesser degree still am.

An electrician appeared at the door. My dad took this stranger in and treated him like a royal guest. I watched as my dad talked to this man in a gentle joking manner. He was a great host. But every time my mother said something, he was sharp and ill-tempered. He was angry, frustrated and quite a bastard as he boomed at her. He turned down the volume and increased the kindness when he answered the electrician's questions.

The anger and sadness rose in me during those moments to heights I had never known. I realized how angry I was at my father for treating my mother like a dog. I remembered that had been the way he'd treated her all my life, as well as me, my sister and my brother. He'd treat a stranger with more kindness than his own family.

Dad kept yelling at my mother and kept being kind to the electrician. I almost had to leave. I wanted to kick him around that small house like I'd kicked and hit pillows in Dan's office, letting out my childhood anger.

Finally the electricity was on and the electrician left. But a light came on inside me, a light that lit up the darkness in which I had often found myself. The last time Dad had said something unkind to my mother, I saw myself in him. In those moments Laural was my mother, and I realized that the way he was behaving with her was exactly the way I would behave with Laural in similar circumstances. Strangers would come to my home and I could treat them with more kindness and compassion than I could the woman I loved and lived with. I saw where I had learned this and was sad and angry at the same time. Mom loved Dad; Laural loved me.

I was my father. With that thought, I started crying.

"What's the matter, Son?" Dad asked, smiling now that his home was intact.

"I hate what you do to Mom," I began my tirade, my anger liberated. "You treated mother like a goddamn dog and you treated that electrician like God. You've always done that to your whole family. You treat a stranger better than the woman you love and have made love to thousands of times and who's cooked for you and cleaned up your messes. And I'm just like you. I treated Laural much the same way and you showed me how. I treated Laural, the woman who loved me more than anybody, the same way you treat Mom."

*He cannot be a man without knowing how to be*
*aggressive,*
*but it must be controlled aggressions that is at*
*his conscious disposal.*
*If he is just overcome by his rage and violence,*
*then it is no good;*
*his masculinity is not yet found.*

Robert Johnson

I knew that Mom and Laural had played their parts in all this, but then it was time to get my anger out for having learned to be the way he was.

"Your Mom understands I love her. Don't you, Baby?" Dad looked at her.

"How would she know?" I said, "You've always treated her like a second-class person."

The dialogue was steady. I was shaking, crying and angry. Dad and I almost came to blows several times. The anger and the tears filled the room. The three of us talked and talked. I told my dad how much I hated him for some of the things I'd seen growing up. And once I got those things out, I told him how much I loved him and loved the good ways I was like him. We held each other and cried and talked for five hours. He asked questions about me and my work as a teacher and counselor. He asked me what I believed and what I felt. We explored each other, and we listened, really listened.

"Dad, I've been trying to write a book about all of this and I'm afraid that I can't."

"Why can't you? What's the book about?"

"It's about me, my life and my changes. It's about you, Mom, Laural and little bits about a teacher of mine named Robert Bly, and Dan Jones and others."

"Sounds like it will help a lot of people, won't it?" Dad asked.

"Yeah, I think so," I responded.

"Then write it," he fired back the order.

"Dad, I can't."

"Why can't you?"

I started crying and realized that I was having as much trouble telling him what was inside me and how I really felt about him as I always did when I tried to tell Laural how much I loved her. Dad looked at me and Mom, who was still crying from listening to us talk and was now looking at me.

"Jimmy, he just can't write the book," Mom offered.

"No, Mom, that is not it. I can write it but I'm afraid to."

"Son, what are you afraid of?" Dad asked patiently.

I sat there crying for four or five minutes and then the words came out with a flood of tears.

"Dad, I'm afraid to write this book because I'm afraid it's going to hurt you, and I don't want to hurt you. I'm afraid that you'll get hurt and angry about what I'm going to say. And I'm afraid that if you do, I'll lose you again. I've been looking for you all my life. I lost you five minutes after I was born and I've needed you for 34 years. Now I've got you. We talk; we hold each other. Dad, I don't want to lose you again. I love you so much. If the book will cost me you, I just can't write it. I need you, Dad, more than I need to write a book."

Dad was crying; Mom was crying and I was bawling like a baby. "Son, as long as you don't say anything bad about your mother, you can write anything you want to about me. I know I failed you as a father. I know that and I'm sorry. But your mother was the best mother in the world. And there's nothing bad that I'll ever let be said about her. I know I've treated you and her and the others bad, so say anything you need to about me."

"Dad, I have to tell the truth about both you and me. Mom made many mistakes. She didn't do everything right either."

"That's right, Jimmy. He's right," my mother broke in.

"No damn it. He's not right. You didn't do anything wrong; I did. But you were the best mother a woman could be, and I won't stand by and let anyone say differently. Son, you can say what you have to about me, but if you have to say anything that will hurt your mother then don't write the book."

"See, Dad, that's why I can't write the book. Because I have to say things that you're not going to like and I don't want to lose you."

"Tell me one thing that your mother did wrong. Just one thing."

"Dad, she smothered me. You were never around so she made up for it with me. And since you weren't there for her, she always expected me to be."

"Well, that's just human. That was a mistake. She was doing the best she knew how." Dad looked at Mom quickly.

"I know, Dad, but it's things like that that caused me some problems, especially with women. I've got to talk about those things and others. I've got to tell the truth, as I see it, about all of us for the book to be of any real help to anyone."

Dad took Mom's hand. "Son," Dad smiled as the tears stood in his eyes, "Write the book. Tell the truth. Say what you need to say about me and your mother. I'll stay with you no matter what you say. She did the best she could and I — well . . ."

"Dad, you did, too."

"Son. Write the book. When you finish it we'll all read it together, and if there're things I don't understand or agree with, we'll talk about it. But I support what you're doing and I'll stand by you all the way."

We all wept and held each other for some time. I had received the blessing I had come for. I was closer to my parents and to writing a book I had been avoiding for more than a year. Now all I had left was to let Laural go. The next day I left for Austin, and knew I was taking my dad and my mom with me and yet also knowing that I had separated from them. I was no longer their child, but a man. Both feelings were wonderful.

# 11 LETTING GO

*He who grasps loses.*

Lao Tzu

The ending circles back to the beginning like the snake eating its own tail. It's difficult to distinguish beginning from end. Much of the same resistance to writing the first chapter of this book reappeared again. I waited patiently, giving myself time to think and feel before beginning.

I had a dream early one morning in which I was released from a prison I had been trying to escape from in dreams for years. The prisons were always different, but that morning I was finally freed after having been in them since I was five or six.

Then I was free to complete this book and close a chapter of my life and a part of my relationship with Laural.

The last several months have been the best of my life. I have been free of depression for over a year now. I have a healthy relationship with my father and mother. I have many men friends as well as women friends whom I love and who love me deeply. I have a growing counseling practice that is teaching and fulfilling me. And I have let Laural go. Yet I know with every fiber of my being that I love her and that she is still with me in my body, memory and spirit, just as my mother and father will always be.

Since January of 1986, I have found myself constantly learning to let go of everyone. Letting go is the central teaching I have found to be the common thread that runs through all religions and is the single greatest task before us. We must constantly learn and relearn how to let go.

I began this year relearning this teaching. It really began in March. Spring brought not only a confirmation of rebirth, but a deep recognition that all the people I had held onto tightly had to be released. It began with the men and women who had been essential to my healing in the last year or two.

The three men who had been my father figures during the course of this transformation period had to cease to be fathers. I had to release them and join them as equals just as I finally did with my own father.

First was Dan Jones. I had recovered my father due in part to this man's help. He helped me release my anger and rage at my father and mother. Dan taught me many things, and I felt like a student, client, nephew and son. In March we decided to jointly lead a men's Gestalt therapy and support group. We would combine forces, strengths and backgrounds to help men break out of destructive and unwanted patterns and help them deal with anger, rage and grief. In order to do this successfully, I had to give up my adolescent need for a father/uncle and become an equal . . . an adult. I did. I let Dan go. We have a wonderful partnership and complement each other's work.

Next I had to let go of my writing mentor, Bill Stott. I had looked to him for childlike guidance for two years. As an elder, he nurtured me. Eventually he became involved enough with my life and ideas to join the men's group I was leading, and to put himself in the position of being counseled by me. After the first group session he volunteered his time and expert writing skills to coauthor this book with me.

I accepted, knowing he was subtly telling me I was now an equal and no longer his student/son. At first we worked together, but we both soon realized that I had to write it alone. We became good friends as I let one more father figure go.

Then came Robert Bly. He was my spiritual father if ever I've had one. But I had to let him go as well. It came one day in a counseling session. I had been talking about Bly's work for four years. After having met him and going through much of what he discussed in his workshops, I was especially touting the work of this father figure. I was a Bly devotee. I didn't want this and I knew he wouldn't. But I was beginning to take Bly's theories and ideas and force-feed them to my clients and make them fit whether they did or not. I stopped before I got myself and my clients in a theoretical straitjacket.

One day during a session, my client said that he had read the interviews I had given him on Bly, and he didn't agree with many things Bly said and didn't quite understand other things. All of a sudden the words, "Bly lives in Minnesota and we're here; this is just you and me, Bill. Let's get to work," came out of my mouth. I couldn't believe I had said that, and at that exact moment I knew I had let Bly go.

That same month I faced the fact that I had to let go of my mother figures. Dr. Mary Mason, my therapist, told me she was preparing to leave the country on a Fulbright Scholarship at the end of April. While she and I had kept a respectable therapeutic distance from each other, I knew she had been one of the most important people in my life during the two years of therapy. But I was ready to terminate my therapy with her after having given myself the gift of continuing to see her long after I was out of crisis. It was during those months prior to her leaving that some of the best work was done.

About this same time my best friend and confidante, Marilyn Yank, began following up on her plans to leave Austin. Marilyn and I had been like brother and sister, and she had seen me through incredibly difficult, if not suicidal, times. Our relationship deepened as trust increased. Space does not allow me to say how much she meant, but she too had to leave and I had to let go.

Finally, during the month of April, I knew it was time to really let Laural go. By letting the father figures and the mother figures go, I knew that I was simultaneously separating finally from my own father and mother and truly becoming an adult in all the ways I had not been. But there was increasing difficulty as I moved from Dr. Mason to Marilyn to Laural. It took two years to let Laural go.

My therapy practice is flourishing. I cut loose from U.T. and the doctorate I didn't want or need. Life was getting better and better, and the only bitter part was the fact that I was still not able to write this book because I had not let Laural go. This meant that I had not reached the place of letting something higher in me move, although I had certainly removed many barriers in the process.

Spring signaled the final separations. I decided to drive to a place in my past that had been calling to me for some time. It was a very special, secret place in the Texas hill country where Laural had once taken me. I had tried to find it once after Laural and I had broken up, but I couldn't. Something in me knew I'd find it this time though it had been a full four years since she had shown it to me. I parked and began walking. I soon came upon it. The spot where we found the cool flowing water. I remembered us taking off our clothes and sitting glistening in the sun on a tree branch that slanted over the spring.

There at that spot I let her go. I sent prayers and messages to God and asked for forgiveness and release from the leftover guilt I carried. I wept for some time, feeling that I had finally let her go, but I was just a little afraid that I was just playing another game. I had thought I had let her go many times before but in actuality had not. However, I was always coming closer to my own center in search of the true ability to love and let go at the same time.

I walked away from this special place knowing something. As I came upon the point where the spring enters the river, I waited. Suddenly out of nowhere a husky bounded down the ridge. I hugged him and held him and thanked him for his power and his presence. I said goodbye to the dog, to the wolf he represented, and inwardly to my relationship with Laural, and walked on.

March turned to April. Dr. Mason was getting ready to leave and was convinced that my therapy with her was complete and a circle had been closed. My friend Marilyn was getting ready to leave for New Mexico, and Laural was making plans to leave the country for a few months. And I was happy, healthy and ready to write my book. I had received my father's blessing, separated from him and my mother, and was more able to love them, others and myself than ever before. The anger was almost totally gone. I had grieved, though often I was still sad over losing Laural. The last week of April I sat down and wrote the first chapter for what would be the seventh time. I knew as I was writing that I had let Laural go.

I wept on the paper and penned my memories, pain and growth. I kept crying and writing, and hours later I completed the first chapter. I knew that I had written it the way I had always wanted to but couldn't because I had not yet let go. Deep down I knew that I had finally stepped out from behind my wall of fear and found myself willing to tell you who I am as truthfully as possible, so that I might further heal myself and perhaps contribute some small amount to your own healing, and maybe Laural's, in the process.

I gave the chapter to Bill Stott, who had been reading everything I had written for two years and urging me to honestly tell my story from my heart. I left him a copy and saw him a week later. He still had not had time to read it and he was leaving the next day for Europe. I left a little disappointed. That evening he called and told me something I had wanted to hear all my adult life. "John, I just read the first chapter. In a word, terrific."

I couldn't believe my ears. My writing at best could have been described as adequate or not too bad. But whether Chapter One was terrific or not was not the issue. What was wonderful that day was that I had known it was good because it was the truth; I knew I could finally divulge my feelings and my truth to my father, the woman I loved and the reader. Thanking Bill for reading it before he left and for his kind

*Goethe came to the
astounding observation late in his life
that the province of man is to
serve woman; then
she will serve him. He was talking about the
inner woman, the muse.*

Robert Johnson

comments, I got off the phone, sat down and wept for half an hour, knowing I had really let Laural go.

So the book is almost completed. I only have a few more things to share with you. I have to tell you how I feel now about Laural, about my work and about myself. I'll keep it short and honest. I have mourned my wounds and no longer inflict them on others. I understand the grief my father felt and could not express. I finally see Laural not as a mother or a superconscious person, but simply as a beautiful woman who knew how to love long before I did. While she has her own wounds to heal, I know now that what she did for me in these last couple of years was hard and easy at the same time. It was difficult to be around me, because she received little comfort and love from me. It seemed to me it was easy for her to do what she was naturally good at doing all along: unconditional loving. But, it took her leaving and my grieving and releasing anger to get me out of the air and into the world of working men.

I still have my issues and problems and I always will. Nevertheless I feel whole and separate from Laural, Mom, Dad, Bly and others even though I love them all more than ever. And although I will no longer be depressed or die if I never see Laural again, I know I will be happy and forever her spiritual friend and brother if never lover and mate.

Last night I had a dream that I have dreamed some version of for 15 or more years — at least as long as I have been consciously remembering and recording my dreams. I was always a prisoner in a cell that contained a few others. I have spent many nights trying to escape. I would weave intricate plans to break out. I'd use manipulative tactics and even force in order to be free. Last night I dreamed I was trying to keep my sanity, and the only way I could do so was by helping others keep their sanity. Finally, at the point where sanity and insanity, freedom and bondage, men and women become indistinct and seem to merge, I heard voices outside the prison door. The only thing I had to do to be free was to walk to the door and gently pull it open. The first thought I had was that the door may have been unlocked for a long time. I asked the people standing outside the prison door what

year it was and discovered I had been a prisoner for 31 years.
I was a very old man. I went back in and saw Laural as an old
woman sitting on the prison bench, and I realized she'd been
with me since the beginning of time. I said to her, "Laural, I
love you and I want to marry you. Now I am free."

# EPILOGUE

It's been almost six months since the dream. While sitting at my writing table, I realized that an empty house has turned into a temple to celebrate the wedding of the goddess Peace and the god Passion. The other morning, I felt something rising in me. It took me several minutes to identify the feeling. It was happiness. I realized that I was now happy and peaceful without Laural by my side. Yet I feel myself to be a passionate man; full of passion for myself, my work, my friends, my planet and someday, when it is time, another love.

Much has happened in the last six months — a lot of work, tears, joy and laughter. I have not seen or heard from Laural for four of those months. During this time I realized that I still had not let Laural go as fully as I needed, and we had not fully forgiven each other. I also realized that I would always love her and she would always love me, but I know that she had lost respect for me years ago. I believe a woman cannot and should not stay with a man she can't respect, no matter how much she loves him. I understand that now and I have

tried, in a nonstriving way, to regain Laural's respect by fully
letting her go, leaving her alone, while silently praying for
her peace and happiness as I learn how to really be a friend.

Now you have finished reading my story and for that I
thank you. Now it is time to go deeper into your own wounds
and heal them so that you too can achieve happiness and
health. Know that you are not alone on your journey.
Together men and women are healing themselves and each
other all across the country. Men's groups similar to the ones
Dan and I lead are springing up like flowers from San
Francisco to Boston. Robert Bly's "Wild Man" workshops
have been drawing phenomenal numbers of men as he helps
take them into their wounds and grief. Like myself, there are
other psychotherapists specializing in masculine psychology
and men's issues; men's books, magazines and newsletters
are appearing daily. Men's centers are available (one soon to
open in Austin) where men can go to listen, talk and work
with other men in a supportive environment. Women are
supporting men in this movement. They fully appreciate the
courage and commitment it takes to gather and help each
other deal with their pain.

While there is much work to be done — there is much
being done and numerous resources you can draw on to
facilitate your healing process. By blending the healing tools
from our culture with others, by synthesizing body/mind/
spiritual therapies and guides, you too can be healed. There
is another place other than the one you've been. It is a place
where the feminine is beautiful, nurturing, strong and gentle,
where the feminine respects and loves the masculine. That
place is inside of you, and you have been journeying there all
your life.

I support you and encourage you to take the next step.
Although that step is scary and the demon that guards the
door separating you from your dreams and goals appears
treacherous — he's not — he's just a fear. Laugh at him and
he will disappear. "Knock and it shall be opened." On the
other side is a place where we can forgive each other and
ourselves, where ". . . man and woman (sic) freed of all false
feelings and reluctances will seek each other not as

opposites, but as brother and sister, as neighbors, and will come together as human beings," (Rilke).

We, can go together. I'll see you there.

# AUSTIN MEN'S CENTER

*A Safe Place for Men, Women and Children*
Director: John Lee

We of the Austin Men's Center integrate psychological, physical and spiritual approaches to growth, change and recovery. A holistic philosophy is used in the care and treatment of individuals who engage in the center's services. The staff, including both men and women, works with men, women and children because the issues of one's sex and age cannot be dealt with in isolation.

Specializations include: Men's Issues and Masculine Psychology, Addictive Relationships and Addictions in general, Co-dependency, Adult Children from Dysfunctional Families and Incest Survivors.

We use a combination of counseling, Gestalt, bio-energetics, Jungian, deep tissue body work (including Rolfing, Shiatsu and Trager massage), dream work, nutritional counseling, marital arts and yoga.

The Center is a focal point for ongoing support groups and information on the Men's Movement and Adult Children work around the country.

Austin Men's Center is also the home of the Primary Emotional Energy Recovery (PEER) Training Program. This training is for counselors and therapists who want to more fully bring the body and the emotions back into the recovery process. The PEER program, an excellent system for accessing and discharging grief and anger, is conducted by John Lee, Dan Jones (Ph.D.) and staff.

For more information write to Austin Men's Center, 700 West Avenue, Austin, Texas, 78701. Phone: (512) 477-9595.

A cassette tape series is available from John Lee at the above address. In a powerful and humorous way, these tapes help you make sense out of the emotional confusion caused by growing up in an alcoholic or dysfunctional family. Titles include:

**Why Men Can't Feel The Price Women Pay**
**Expressing Anger Appropriately**
**Grieving, A Key To Healing**
**Healing The Father-Son Wound**
**What Co-dependency Really Is**
**Addictive Relationships**
**Saying Goodbye To Mom And Dad**
**The Flying Boy: Healing The Wounded Man Workshop**
(3 tapes at $24.95 plus $2.50 for postage/handling)

- Tapes are $9.95 each plus $1.95 for postage/handling.
- A set of any 4 tapes is $29.95 plus $2.50 postage/handling.
- Buy any 6 tapes for $49.95 plus $3.50 postage/handling, and receive a 7th tape FREE.
- Texas residents add 8% sales tax.

# Other Books By . . .

# HEALTH COMMUNICATIONS, INC.

Enterprise Center
3201 Southwest 15th Street
Deerfield Beach, FL 33442
Phone: 800-851-9100

*ADULT CHILDREN OF ALCOHOLICS*
Janet Woititz
Over a year on The New York Times Best Seller list,this book is the primer on Adult Children of Alcoholics.
**ISBN 0-932194-15-X** $6.95

*STRUGGLE FOR INTIMACY*
Janet Woititz
Another best seller, this book gives insightful advice on learning to love more fully.
**ISBN 0-932194-25-7** $6.95

*DAILY AFFIRMATIONS: For Adult Children of Alcoholics*
Rokelle Lerner
These positive affirmations for every day of the year paint a mental picture of your life as you choose it to be.
**ISBN 0-932194-27-3** $6.95

*CHOICEMAKING: For Co-dependents, Adult Children and Spirituality Seekers* — Sharon Wegscheider-Cruse
This useful book defines the problems and solves them in a positive way.
**ISBN 0-932194-26-5** $9.95

*LEARNING TO LOVE YOURSELF: Finding Your Self-Worth*
Sharon Wegscheider-Cruse
"Self-worth is a choice, not a birthright", says the author as she shows us how we can choose positive self-esteem.
**ISBN 0-932194-39-7** $7.95

*LET GO AND GROW: Recovery for Adult Children*
Robert Ackerman
An in-depth study of the different characteristics of adult children of alcoholics with guidelines for recovery.
**ISBN 0-932194-51-6** $8.95

*LOST IN THE SHUFFLE: The Co-dependent Reality*
Robert Subby
A look at the unreal rules the co-dependent lives by and the way out of the dis-eased reality.
**ISBN 0-932194-45-1** $8.95

# New Books . . .
## from Health Communications

*BRADSHAW ON: THE FAMILY: A Revolutionary Way of Self-Discovery*
John Bradshaw
The host of the nationally televised series of the same name shows us how families can be healed and we as individuals can realize our full potential.
**ISBN 0-932194-54-0** $9.95

*HEALING THE CHILD WITHIN: Discovery and Recovery for Adult Children of Dysfunctional Families* — Charles Whitfield
Dr. Whitfield defines, describes and discovers how we can reach our Child Within to heal and nurture our woundedness.
**ISBN 0-932194-40-0** $8.95

*WHISKY'S SONG: An Explicit Story of Surviving in an Alcoholic Home*
Mitzi Chandler
A beautiful but brutal story of growing up where violence and neglect are everyday occurrences conveys a positive message of survival and love.
**ISBN 0-932194-42-7** $6.95

# New Books on Spiritual Recovery . . .
## from Health Communications

*THE JOURNEY WITHIN: A Spiritual Path to Recovery*
Ruth Fishel
This book will lead you from your dysfunctional beginnings to the place within where renewal occurs.
**ISBN 0-932194-41-9** $8.95

*LEARNING TO LIVE IN THE NOW: 6-Week Personal Plan To Recovery*
Ruth Fishel
The author gently introduces you to the valuable healing tools of meditation, positive creative visualization and affirmations.
**ISBN 0-932194-62-1** $7.95

*GENESIS: Spirituality in Recovery for Co-dependents*
by Julie D. Bowden and Herbert L. Gravitz
A self-help spiritual program for adult children of trauma, an in-depth look at "turning it over" and "letting go".
**ISBN 0-932194-56-7** $6.95

*GIFTS FOR PERSONAL GROWTH AND RECOVERY*
Wayne Kritsberg
Gifts for healing which include journal writing, breathing, positioning and meditation.
**ISBN 0-932194-60-5** $6.95